THE WHO'S BUYING SERIES
BY THE NEW STRATEGIST EDITORS

Who's Buying Information Products and Services

2nd EDITION

New Strategist Publications, Inc.
P.O. Box 242, Ithaca, New York 14851
800/848-0842; 607/273-0913
www.newstrategist.com

Copyright 2005. NEW STRATEGIST PUBLICATIONS, INC.

All rights reserved.

No part of this book may be reproduced, stored in a retrieval system, or transmitted in any form or by any means, electronic, mechanical, photocopying, microfilming, recording, or otherwise without written permission from the Publisher.

ISBN 1-885070-96-9

Printed in the United States of America

Contents

About the Data in Who's Buying Information Products and Services 5
1. Percent Reporting Expenditure and Amount Spent, Average Quarter 2003 9

Household Spending Trends: 2000 to 2003 10
2. Household Spending Trends, 2000 to 2003 11

Household Spending on Information Products and Services, 2003 14
3. Information Products and Services: Spending, 2000 and 2003 16

Household Spending on Information Products and Services by Demographic Characteristic, 2003
4. Information Products and Services: Average Spending by Age, 2003 17
5. Information Products and Services: Indexed Spending by Age, 2003 18
6. Information Products and Services: Total Spending by Age, 2003 19
7. Information Products and Services: Market Shares by Age, 2003 20
8. Information Products and Services: Average Spending by Income, 2003 21
9. Information Products and Services: Indexed Spending by Income, 2003 22
10. Information Products and Services: Total Spending by Income, 2003 23
11. Information Products and Services: Market Shares by Income, 2003 24
12. Information Products and Services: Average Spending
    by High-Income Consumer Units, 2003 25
13. Information Products and Services: Indexed Spending
    by High-Income Consumer Units, 2003 26
14. Information Products and Services: Total Spending
    by High-Income Consumer Units, 2003 27
15. Information Products and Services: Market Shares
    by High-Income Consumer Units, 2003 28
16. Information Products and Services: Average Spending by Household Type, 2003 29
17. Information Products and Services: Indexed Spending by Household Type, 2003 30
18. Information Products and Services: Total Spending by Household Type, 2003 31
19. Information Products and Services: Market Shares by Household Type, 2003 32
20. Information Products and Services: Average Spending
    by Race and Hispanic Origin, 2003 33
21. Information Products and Services: Indexed Spending
    by Race and Hispanic Origin, 2003 34
22. Information Products and Services: Total Spending by Race and Hispanic Origin, 2003 35
23. Information Products and Services: Market Shares by Race and Hispanic Origin, 2003 36
24. Information Products and Services: Average Spending by Region, 2003 37
25. Information Products and Services: Indexed Spending by Region, 2003 38
26. Information Products and Services: Total Spending by Region, 2003 39
27. Information Products and Services: Market Shares by Region, 2003 40
28. Information Products and Services: Average Spending by Education, 2003 41
29. Information Products and Services: Indexed Spending by Education, 2003 42
30. Information Products and Services: Total Spending by Education, 2003 43
31. Information Products and Services: Market Shares by Education, 2003 44

Household Spending on Information Products and Services by Product Category, 2003

32. Books (Except Those Purchased through Book Clubs) 46
33. Books Purchased through Book Clubs 48
34. Cable TV or Community Antenna 50
35. Cellular Phone Service 52
36. Computers and Computer Hardware for Nonbusiness Use 54
37. Computer Information Services 56
38. Computer Software and Accessories for Nonbusiness Use 58
39. Magazines, Nonsubscription 60
40. Magazine Subscriptions 62
41. Newspapers, Nonsubscription 64
42. Newspaper Subscriptions 66
43. Phone Cards 68
44. Residential Telephone Service and Pay Phones 70
45. Telephones, Answering Machines, and Accessories 72
46. Televison Sets 74

Appendix: Spending by Product and Service, 2003 Ranking 76

Glossary 83

About the data in Who's Buying Information Products and Services

Introduction

The spending data in *Who's Buying Information Products and Services* are based on the Bureau of Labor Statistics' Consumer Expenditure Survey, an ongoing, nationwide survey of household spending. The Consumer Expenditure Survey is a complete accounting of household expenditures, including everything from big-ticket items, such as homes and cars, to small purchases like laundry detergent and videos. The survey does not include expenditures by government, business, or institutions. The lag time between data collection and dissemination is about two years. The data in this report are from the 2003 Consumer Expenditure Survey, unless otherwise noted.

To produce this report, New Strategist Publications analyzed the Consumer Expenditure Survey's average household spending data in a variety of ways, calculating household spending indexes, aggregate (or total) household spending, and market shares. Spending data by age, household income, household type, race, Hispanic origin, region, and education are shown in this report. These analyses are presented in two formats—for all product categories by demographic characteristic and for all demographic characteristics by product category.

Definition of consumer unit

The Consumer Expenditure Survey uses the consumer unit rather than the household as the sampling unit. The term "household" is used interchangeably with the term "consumer unit" in this report for convenience, although they are not exactly the same. Some households contain more than one consumer unit.

The Bureau of Labor Statistics defines consumer unit as either (1) members of a household who are related by blood, marriage, adoption, or other legal arrangements; (2) a person living alone or sharing a household with others or living as a roomer in a private home or lodging house or in permanent living quarters in a hotel or motel, but who is financially independent; or (3) two persons or more living together who pool their income to make joint expenditure decisions. The bureau defines financial independence in terms of "the three major expenses categories: housing, food, and other living expenses. To be considered financially independent, at least two of the three major expense categories have to be provided by the respondent."

The Census Bureau uses household as its sampling unit in the decennial census and in the monthly Current Population Survey. The Census Bureau's household "consists of all persons who occupy a housing unit. A house, an apartment or other groups of rooms, or a single room is regarded as a housing unit when it is occupied or intended for occupancy as separate living quarters; that is, when the occupants do not live and eat with any other persons in the structure and there is direct access from the outside or through a common hall." The definition goes on to specify that "a household includes the related family members and all the unrelated persons, if any, such as lodgers, foster children, wards, or employees who share the housing unit. A person living alone in a housing unit or a group of unrelated persons sharing a housing unit as partners is also counted as a household. The count of households excludes group quarters."

Because there can be more than one consumer unit in a household, consumer units outnumber households by several million. Young adults under age 25 head most of the additional consumer units.

How to use the tables in this report

The starting point for all calculations are the unpublished, detailed average household spending data collected by the Consumer Expenditure Survey. These numbers are shown on the report's average spending tables and on each of the product-specific tables. New Strategist's editors calculated the other figures in the report based on the average figures. The indexed spending tables and the indexed spending column (Best Customers) on the product-specific tables reveal whether spending by households in a given segment is above or below the average for all households and by how much. The total (or aggregate) spending tables show the overall size of the market. The market share tables and market share column (Biggest Customers) on the product-specific tables reveal how much spending each household segment controls. These analyses are described in detail below.

• **Average Spending.** The average spending figures show the average annual spending of households on information products and services in 2003. The Consumer Expenditure Survey produces average spending data for all households in a segment, e.g., all households with a householder aged 25 to 34, not just for those purchasing an item. When examining spending data, it is important to remember that by including both purchasers and nonpurchasers in the calculation, the average is less than the amount spent on the item by buyers. (See table 1 for the percentage of households that spent on information products and services in 2003 and how much the purchasers spent.)

Because average spending figures include both buyers and nonbuyers, they reveal spending patterns by demographic characteristic. By knowing who is most likely to spend on an item, marketers can target their advertising and promotions more efficiently, and businesses can determine the market potential of a product or service in a city or neighborhood. By multiplying the average amount households spend on computer information services by the number of households in an area, for example, an Internet service provider can estimate the potential size of the local market for online services.

• **Indexed Spending (Best Customers).** The indexed spending figures compare the spending of each household segment with that of the average household. To compute the indexes, New Strategist divides the average amount each household segment spends on an item by average household spending, and multiplying the resulting figure by 100.

An index of 100 is the average for all households. An index of 125 means the spending of a household segment is 25 percent above average (100 plus 25). An index of 75 indicates spending that is 25 percent below the average for all households (100 minus 25). Indexed spending figures identify the best customers for a product or service. Households with an index of 178 for cell phone service, for example, are a strong market for this service. Those with an index below 100 are either a weak or an underserved market.

Spending indexes can reveal hidden markets—household segments with a high propensity to buy a particular product or service but which are overshadowed by household segments that account for a larger share of the market. Householders aged 35 to 44, for example, account for 22 percent of the book market—a larger share than the 20 percent controlled by householders aged 55 to 64. But a look at the indexed spending figures reveals that, in fact, the older householders are the best customers. Householder aged 55 to 64 spend 36 percent more than the average household on books, while those aged 35 to 44 spend only 2 percent more than average. Booksellers can use this information to target their best customers.

Note that because of sampling errors, small differences in index values may not be significant. But the broader patterns revealed by indexes can guide marketers to the best customers.

- **Total (Aggregate) Spending.** To produce the total (aggregate) spending figures, New Strategist multiplies average spending by the number of households in a segment. The result is the dollar size of the total household market and of each market segment. All totals are shown in thousands of dollars. To convert the numbers in the total spending tables to dollars, you must append "000" to the number. For example, households headed by people aged 35 to 44 spent more than $9 billion ($9,261,072,000) on cell phone service in 2003.

When comparing the total spending figures in this report with total spending estimates from the Bureau of Economic Analysis, other government agencies, or trade associations, keep in mind that the Consumer Expenditure Survey includes only household spending, not spending by businesses or institutions. Sales data also will differ from household spending totals because sales figures for consumer products include the value of goods sold to industries, government, and foreign markets, which can be a significant proportion of sales.

- **Market Shares (Biggest Customers).** New Strategist produces market share figures by converting total (aggregate) spending data into percentages. To calculate the percentage of total spending on an item that is controlled by a demographic segment—i.e., its market share—the segment's total spending on an item is divided by aggregate household spending on the item.

Market shares reveal the biggest customers—the demographic segments that account for the largest share of spending on a particular product or service. In 2003, for example, householders aged 55 or older accounted for 55 percent of spending on newspaper subscriptions. By targeting only older householders, newspaper publishers could reach the majority of their customers. There's a danger here, however. By single-mindedly targeting the biggest customers, businesses cannot nurture potential growth markets. With competition for customers more heated than ever, targeting potential markets is increasingly important to business survival.

- **Product-Specific Tables.** The product-specific tables reveal at a glance the demographic characteristics of spending by individual product category. These tables show average spending, indexed spending (Best Customers), and market shares (Biggest Customers) by age, income, household type, race and Hispanic origin, region, and education. If you want to see the spending pattern for an individual product at a glance, these are the tables for you.

History and methodology of the Consumer Expenditure Survey

The Consumer Expenditure Survey (CEX) is an ongoing study of the day-to-day spending of American households. In taking the survey, government interviewers collect spending data on products and services as well as the amount and sources of household income, changes in savings and debt, and demographic and economic characteristics of household members. The Bureau of the Census collects data for the CEX under contract with the Bureau of Labor Statistics (BLS), which is responsible for analysis and release of the survey data.

Since the late 19th century, the federal government has conducted expenditure surveys about every ten years. Although the results have been used for a variety of purposes, their primary application is to track consumer prices. In 1980, the CEX became a continuous survey with annual release of data (with a lag time of about two years between data collection and release). The survey is used to update prices for the market basket of products and services used in calculating the Consumer Price Index.

The CEX consists of two separate surveys: an interview survey and a diary survey. In the interview portion of the survey, respondents are asked each quarter for five consecutive quarters to report their expenditures for the previous three months. The purchase of big-ticket items, such as houses, cars, and major appliances, and recurring expenses such as insurance premiums, utility payments, and rent are recorded by the interview survey. About 95 percent of all expenditures are covered by the interview component.

Expenditures on small, frequently purchased items are recorded during a two-week period by the diary survey. These detailed records include expenses for food and beverages purchased in grocery stores and at restaurants, as well as other items such as tobacco, housekeeping supplies, nonprescription drugs, and personal care products and services. The diary survey is intended to capture expenditures respondents are likely to forget or recall incorrectly over longer periods of time.

Two separate, nationally representative samples are used for the interview and diary surveys. For the interview survey, about 7,500 consumer units are interviewed on a rotating panel basis each quarter for five consecutive quarters. Another 7,500 consumer units keep weekly diaries of spending for two consecutive weeks. Data collection is carried out in 105 areas of the country.

The data are reviewed, audited, and cleaned by the BLS, and then weighted to reflect the number and characteristics of all U.S. consumer units. Like any sample survey, the CEX is subject to two major types of error. Nonsampling error occurs when respondents misinterpret questions or interviewers are inconsistent in the way they ask questions or record answers. Respondents may forget items, recall expenses incorrectly, or deliberately give wrong answers. A respondent may remember how much he or she spent at the grocery store but forget the items picked up at a local convenience store. Nonsampling error can also be caused by mistakes during the various stages of data processing and refinement.

Sampling error occurs when a sample does not accurately represent the population it is supposed to represent. This kind of error is present in every sample-based survey and is minimized by using a proper sampling procedure. Standard error tables documenting the extent of sampling error in the CEX are available from the BLS at http://www.bls.gov/cex/csxstnderror.htm.

Although the CEX is the best source of information about the spending behavior of American households, it should be treated with caution because of the above problems.

For more information

To find out more about the Consumer Expenditure Survey, contact the CEX specialists at the Bureau of Labor Statistics at (202) 691-6900 or visit the CEX home page at http://www.bls.gov/cex/. The web site includes news releases, technical documentation, and current and historical summary-level CEX data. The detailed average spending data shown in this report are available from the BLS only by special request.

For a comprehensive look at detailed household spending data for all products and services, see the tenth edition of *Household Spending: Who Spends How Much on What* available from New Strategist Publications in hardcopy or online at http://www.newstrategist.com or by calling 1-800-848-0842. To download spending reports for individual product and service categories, visit the instant-answer service at http://www.nspend.com.

Table 1. Percent Reporting Expenditure and Amount Spent, Average Quarter 2003

(percent of consumer units reporting expenditure and amount spent by purchasers during an average quarter, 2003)

	average quarter	
	percent reporting expenditure	amount spent by purchasers
Computer		
Computer information services	41.3%	$75.05
Computers and computer hardware, nonbusiness use	4.6	749.84
Computer software and accessories, nonbusiness use	4.1	110.17
Reading material		
Newspaper subscriptions	22.3	46.63
Books (except those purchased through book clubs)	19.4	61.64
Newspapers, nonsubscription	14.1	17.23
Magazines, nonsubscription	10.3	18.84
Magazine subscriptions	8.2	44.22
Books purchased through book clubs	2.5	58.06
Telephone		
Residential telephone service and pay phones	89.5	173.09
Cellular phone service	42.1	187.53
Phone cards	9.9	47.77
Telephones and accessories	4.6	77.03
Television		
Cable service and community antenna	68.9	153.73
Televisions (table model)	2.5	346.50
Televisions (console)	1.0	1,456.19

Note: Expenditures shown are total net outlays at the time of purchase, whether or not the item was financed.
Source: Calculations by New Strategist based on the 2003 Consumer Expenditure Survey

Household Spending Trends: 2000 to 2003

Between 2000 and 2003, spending by the average household barely changed, inching up by just 0.4 percent (or $178) to $40,817, after adjusting for inflation. At the same time, average household income grew a larger 7.2 percent, revealing the caution of consumers during the sluggish economic recovery. The media may claim Americans spend beyond their means, but in fact the steady rise in consumer spending at the national level is primarily the result of demographic change—population growth and the aging of the baby-boom generation into the peak earning and spending years.

The anemic growth in average household spending between 2000 and 2003 should come as no surprise. American households have been cutting their spending on discretionary items for years as nondiscretionary expenses claim an ever-growing share of the household budget. Declines in discretionary spending are evident in the 2000 to 2003 trends. Spending on food away from home (primarily restaurant and take-out meals) fell 3 percent during those years, after adjusting for inflation. Spending on alcoholic beverages shrank 2 percent. Spending on apparel fell an enormous 17 percent, and the average amount devoted to reading material dropped by an even larger 19 percent. Spending on "other lodging," a category that includes hotel and motel expenses, fell 13 percent. Although entertainment spending rose 3.5 percent overall between 2000 and 2003, spending on fees and admissions to entertainment events fell 10 percent.

Americans cut back on many discretionary purchases because their nondiscretionary expenses—the spending they cannot control—was on the rise. After adjusting for inflation, the average household spent 10 percent more on property taxes in 2003 than in 2000. Mortgage interest expenses rose 5 percent despite falling interest rates because of the surge in homeownership. Out-of-pocket spending on health insurance increased 19 percent. Spending on vehicle insurance grew 9 percent. Spending on water and other public services increased 3 percent. Spending on education rose 16 percent.

Contrary to popular perception, Americans are cautious spenders at the individual household level. The recession of 2001 followed by the slow recovery forced households to spend less on discretionary items to make ends meet. Rising energy costs—not yet reflected in these numbers—are likely to reduce discretionary spending even further. With the aging baby-boom generation entering its sixties and exiting the peak spending years, average household spending is likely to remain modest. The U.S. economy will have to adapt. Fortunately, the tools are in hand—there's no better way to prepare for the future than to understand household spending patterns.

Table 2. Household Spending Trends, 2000 to 2003

(average annual spending of consumer units by product and service category, 2000 and 2003; percent change 2000–03; in 2003 dollars)

	2003	2000	percent change 2000–03
Number of consumer units (in 000s)	115,356	109,367	5.5%
Average before-tax income	$51,128	$47,693	7.2
Average annual spending	40,817	40,639	0.4
FOOD	5,340	5,510	–3.1
Food at home	3,129	3,227	–3.0
Cereals and bakery products	442	484	–8.7
Cereals and cereal products	150	167	–10.0
Bakery products	292	317	–8.0
Meats, poultry, fish, and eggs	825	849	–2.9
Beef	246	254	–3.2
Pork	171	178	–4.1
Other meats	102	108	–5.5
Poultry	145	155	–6.4
Fish and seafood	124	118	5.5
Eggs	37	36	1.9
Dairy products	328	347	–5.5
Fresh milk and cream	127	140	–9.2
Other dairy products	201	206	–2.5
Fruits and vegetables	535	557	–3.9
Fresh fruits	171	174	–1.8
Fresh vegetables	172	170	1.3
Processed fruits	108	123	–12.1
Processed vegetables	84	90	–6.4
Other food at home	999	990	0.9
Sugar and other sweets	119	125	–4.8
Fats and oils	86	89	–3.0
Miscellaneous foods	490	467	5.0
Nonalcoholic beverages	268	267	0.4
Food prepared by household on trips	36	43	–15.7
Food away from home	2,211	2,283	–3.1
ALCOHOLIC BEVERAGES	391	397	–1.6
HOUSING	13,432	13,159	2.1
Shelter	7,887	7,599	3.8
Owned dwellings	5,263	4,916	7.1
Mortgage interest and charges	2,954	2,819	4.8
Property taxes	1,344	1,217	10.5
Maintenance, repairs, insurance, other expenses	965	881	9.5
Rented dwellings	2,179	2,173	0.3
Other lodging	445	511	–12.8
Utilities, fuels, and public services	2,811	2,659	5.7
Natural gas	392	328	19.5
Electricity	1,028	973	5.6
Fuel oil and other fuels	110	104	6.2
Telephone services	956	937	2.1
Water and other public services	326	316	3.1
Household services	707	731	–3.2
Personal services	294	348	–15.6
Other household services	414	382	8.3

	2003	2000	percent change 2000–03
Housekeeping supplies	$529	$515	2.7%
Laundry and cleaning supplies	132	140	–5.7
Other household products	263	241	8.9
Postage and stationery	133	135	–1.2
Household furnishings and equipment	1,497	1,655	–9.5
Household textiles	113	113	–0.2
Furniture	401	418	–4.0
Floor coverings	52	47	10.6
Major appliances	196	202	–2.9
Small appliances, miscellaneous housewares	88	93	–5.3
Miscellaneous household equipment	648	781	–17.0
APPAREL AND SERVICES	1,640	1,983	–17.3
Men and boys	372	470	–20.9
Men, aged 16 or older	282	368	–23.3
Boys, aged 2 to 15	89	103	–13.2
Women and girls	634	774	–18.1
Women, aged 16 or older	529	648	–18.4
Girls, aged 2 to 15	106	126	–15.9
Children under age 2	81	88	–7.5
Footwear	294	366	–19.8
Other apparel products and services	258	284	–9.2
TRANSPORTATION	7,781	7,923	–1.8
Vehicle purchases	3,732	3,651	2.2
Cars and trucks, new	2,052	1,714	19.7
Cars and trucks, used	1,611	1,891	–14.8
Gasoline and motor oil	1,333	1,379	–3.3
Other vehicle expenses	2,331	2,437	–4.3
Vehicle finance charges	371	350	5.9
Maintenance and repairs	619	667	–7.1
Vehicle insurance	905	831	8.9
Vehicle rental, leases, licenses, other charges	436	589	–25.9
Public transportation	385	456	–15.6
HEALTH CARE	2,416	2,207	9.5
Health insurance	1,252	1,050	19.2
Medical services	591	607	–2.6
Drugs	467	444	5.1
Medical supplies	107	106	1.2
ENTERTAINMENT	2,060	1,990	3.5
Fees and admissions	494	550	–10.2
Television, radio, sound equipment	730	664	9.9
Pets, toys, and playground equipment	378	357	6.0
Other entertainment supplies, services	457	420	8.9
PERSONAL CARE PRODUCTS AND SERVICES	527	603	–12.5
READING	127	156	–18.6
EDUCATION	783	675	16.0
TOBACCO PRODUCTS AND SMOKING SUPPLIES	290	341	–14.9
MISCELLANEOUS	606	829	–26.9
CASH CONTRIBUTIONS	1,370	1,273	7.6
PERSONAL INSURANCE AND PENSIONS	4,055	3,594	12.8
Life and other personal insurance	397	426	–6.9
Pensions and Social Security	3,658	3,168	15.5
PERSONAL TAXES	2,532	3,330	–24.0
Federal income taxes	1,843	2,573	–28.4
State and local income taxes	502	600	–16.4
Other taxes	187	156	19.9

	2003	2000	percent change 2000–03
GIFTS FOR NONHOUSEHOLD MEMBERS	$1,007	$1,157	–13.0%
Food	78	75	4.3
Alcoholic beverages	16	15	7.0
Housing	220	311	–29.2
Housekeeping supplies	42	42	0.8
Household textiles	13	14	–6.4
Appliances and misc. housewares	25	30	–16.4
Major appliances	7	9	–18.1
Small appliances and misc. housewares	18	22	–19.8
Miscellaneous household equipment	57	75	–23.8
Other housing	85	150	–43.2
Apparel and services	225	261	–13.7
Males, aged 2 or older	56	73	–22.9
Females, aged 2 or older	80	91	–11.9
Children under age 2	39	44	–11.0
Other apparel products and services	50	55	–8.2
Jewelry and watches	26	21	21.7
All other apparel products and services	25	32	–22.0
Transportation	60	75	–19.8
Health care	48	41	18.3
Entertainment	69	100	–31.3
Toys, games, hobbies, and tricycles	26	32	–18.9
Other entertainment	43	68	–37.1
Personal care products and services	16	20	–21.2
Reading	1	2	–53.2
Education	200	161	24.0
All other gifts	74	95	–22.2

Note: The Bureau of Labor Statistics uses consumer unit rather than household as the sampling unit in the Consumer Expenditure Survey. For the definition of consumer unit, see the glossary. Spending by category will not add to total spending because gift spending is also included in the preceding product and service categories and personal taxes are not included in the total. Source: Bureau of Labor Statistics, 2000 and 2003 Consumer Expenditure Surveys, Internet site http://www.bls.gov/cex/home.htm; calculations by New Strategist

Household Spending on Information Products and Services, 2003

Between 2000 and 2003, average household spending on information products and services (computers, telephones, television, and reading material) rose by 5 percent, to $1,909, after adjusting for inflation. This small increase in spending masks sweeping changes in the way households allocate their dollars within the broad information product and service category. Average household spending on reading material fell a steep 18 percent between 2000 and 2003, while spending on television (primarily cable service) rose 25 percent. Spending on telephone products and services climbed just 1 percent, while spending on computers fell 2 percent.

A closer look at spending within each major category reveals how households are responding to far-reaching technological change. The average household more than doubled spending on cellular phone service during the three-year period, after adjusting for inflation. Spending on computer information services (Internet) climbed by 89 percent. But spending on residential phone service fell 23 percent, spending on computer hardware declined 32 percent, and spending on computer software fell 4 percent. Spending on reading material diminished in every individual category. Book spending experienced the smallest decline, with average household spending on books falling 10 percent between 2000 and 2003, after adjusting for inflation. Spending on newspaper subscriptions fell 18 percent, and spending on magazine subscriptions was down a substantial 29 percent.

In 2003 as in 2000, the average household devoted the largest share of its information spending to residential phone service. Residential service accounted for slightly less than one-third of information spending (32.5 percent) in 2003. This figure was sharply lower than the 44 percent share held by residential phone service in 2000, however. Cable service ranked second in both years, but cable's share rose from 19 to 22 percent between 2000 and 2003. Cellular phone service ranked third in 2003, up from fourth in 2000, its share rising from 7 to 17 percent. Computer information services ranked sixth in 2000 and fifth in 2003, its share rising from 4 to 6 percent during those years. Books almost held their ground, with a 2.5 percent share in 2003, down from 2.9 percent in 2000. Every type of reading material lost market share during those years. By 2003, reading material accounted for just 7 percent of household spending on information products and services, down from 9 percent in 2000.

Within information product and service categories, important shifts are taking place. The average household already spends more on computer information services than on computer software. In a few years, spending on computer information services is likely to overtake computer hardware spending as well. In 2000, cellular phone service accounted for just 13 percent of telephone spending. By 2003, the share had climbed to 32 percent. Spending on cellular service could overtake residential phone service in the years ahead as cell phones replace landline phones in the household.

Spending by age

Householders aged 45 to 54 spend the most on information products and services—$2,338 in 2003, or 22 percent more than the average household. A look at spending by detailed category reveals sharp differences in spending patterns by age. Spending on computer information services peaks in the 35-to-54 age group, at 22 to 33 percent above average. Spending on cell phone service skews younger, with spending 19 to 31 percent above average in the 25 to 54 age groups. Older householders dominate spending on reading material. Households headed by people aged 55 or older control 55 percent of spending on newspaper subscriptions. Householders aged 55 to 74 spend 42 to 46 percent more than average on magazine subscriptions, while householders under age 45 spend well below average on this item. These differences in spending by age suggest more change lies ahead as younger Internet and cell phone users replace older print aficionados.

Spending by household income

Not surprisingly, spending on information products and services rises with income in all but one category—spending on phone cards is below average for households with incomes of $50,000 or more. Income makes a big difference on book spending. Households with incomes of $100,000 or more spend more than twice the average on books, accounting for 32 percent of household spending on this item—a much greater proportion than their 12 percent share of households. The affluent spend nearly three times the average on television sets—a category that includes the increasingly popular and expensive wide-screen TVs. Households with incomes of $100,000 or more spend closer to the average on widely used products and services, such as residential phone service (36 percent more than average) and cable service (49 percent more).

Spending by household type

Married couples with school-aged or older children at home devote the largest amount of money to information products and services, spending 30 to 41 percent more than average. Couples with children aged 18 or older at home are the best customers of cell phone service, spending 72 percent more than the average household on this item. Married couples with school-aged or older children at home spend 53 to 57 percent more than average on computer information services. Those without children at home (most of them empty-nesters) spend the most on reading material, particularly newspaper and magazine subscriptions (spending 70 and 66 percent more than average, respectively).

Spending by race and Hispanic origin

Blacks and Hispanics spend slightly less than average on information products and services overall, while Asians and whites spend an average amount. Black and Hispanic spending is well above average on a few items, however. Blacks spend 19 percent more than the average household on residential phone service. Hispanics spend three times the average on phone cards. Asians spend more on computers and books than any other racial or ethnic group.

Spending by region

Spending on information products and services overall does not vary much by region. But by individual category there are some important regional differences. Average household spending on computers is 29 percent above average in the West and 16 percent below average in the South. Spending on reading material is above average in every region except the South, where it is 27 percent below average.

Spending by education

College graduates spend 31 percent more than the average household on information products and services. On some items, however, their spending is not far above average. College graduates spend only 14 percent more than the average household on cable service and only 12 percent more on residential phone service. They spend 10 percent less than average on phone cards. Book spending shows the biggest difference by education. College graduates spend more than twice the average on books, controlling 59 percent of the book market. They spend 51 percent more than average on computer information services and 33 percent more than average on cell phone service.

Table 3. Information Product and Service Spending, 2000 and 2003

(average annual and percent distribution of household spending on information products and services, 2000 and 2003; percent change in spending, 2000–03; in 2003 dollars)

	2003		2000		
	average household spending	percent distribution	average household spending (in 2003$)	percent distribution	percent change 2000–03
INFORMATION SPENDING	$1,908.83	100.0%	$1,825.99	100.0%	4.5%
Telephone	983.41	51.5	970.12	53.1	1.4
Television	515.28	27.0	412.15	22.6	25.0
Computer	282.87	14.8	287.89	15.8	–1.7
Reading material	127.27	6.7	155.83	8.5	–18.3
INFORMATION SPENDING	1,908.83	100.0	1,825.99	100.0	4.5
Residential telephone service and pay phones	619.60	32.5	809.15	44.3	–23.4
Cable service and community antenna	423.79	22.2	343.19	18.8	23.5
Cellular phone service	316.10	16.6	127.68	7.0	147.6
Computers and computer hardware, nonbusiness use	136.77	7.2	200.70	11.0	–31.9
Computer information services	123.92	6.5	65.56	3.6	89.0
Televisions	91.49	4.8	68.96	3.8	32.7
Books (except those purchased through book clubs)	47.81	2.5	52.91	2.9	–9.6
Newspaper subscriptions	41.54	2.2	50.68	2.8	–18.0
Telephones and answering machines	27.71	1.5	33.30	1.8	–16.8
Phone cards	18.88	1.0	–	–	–
Computer software and accessories, nonbusiness use	17.98	0.9	18.69	1.0	–3.8
Magazine subscriptions	14.45	0.8	20.41	1.1	–29.2
Newspapers, nonsubscription	9.71	0.5	13.10	0.7	–25.9
Magazines, nonsubscription	7.73	0.4	10.15	0.6	–23.8
Books purchased through book clubs	5.69	0.3	8.58	0.5	–33.7
Repair of computer systems for nonbusiness use	4.20	0.2	2.94	0.2	42.9

Note: Numbers will not add to total because not all categories are shown. (–) means data are not available.
Source: Bureau of Labor Statistics, 2000 and 2003 Consumer Expenditure Surveys; calculations by New Strategist

Table 4. Information Products and Services: Average spending by age, 2003

(average annual spending of consumer units (CU) on information products and services, by age of consumer unit reference person, 2003)

	total consumer units	under 25	25 to 34	35 to 44	45 to 54	55 to 64	65 to 74	75+
Number of consumer units (000s)	115,356	8,584	19,737	24,413	23,131	16,580	11,495	11,417
Number of persons per CU	2.5	1.8	2.9	3.2	2.6	2.1	1.9	1.5
Average before-tax income of CU	$51,128.00	$20,680.00	$50,389.00	$61,091.00	$68,028.00	$58,672.00	$35,314.00	$25,492.00
Average spending of CU, total	40,817.33	22,395.53	40,525.22	47,175.06	50,100.86	44,190.65	33,629.17	25,016.38
INFORMATION SPENDING	**1,908.83**	**1,137.05**	**1,924.32**	**2,144.23**	**2,337.82**	**2,083.08**	**1,588.32**	**1,159.00**
Computer	**282.87**	**198.09**	**301.09**	**331.20**	**374.30**	**329.08**	**173.38**	**69.69**
Computers and computer hardware, nonbusiness use	136.77	116.14	151.31	153.24	181.26	166.11	71.71	24.67
Computer information services	123.92	63.03	128.82	151.71	165.06	134.86	84.55	42.21
Computer software and accessories, nonbusiness use	17.98	18.07	18.25	20.73	22.12	22.90	12.22	1.83
Repair of computer systems for nonbusiness use	4.20	0.85	2.71	5.52	5.86	5.21	4.90	0.98
Reading material	**127.27**	**52.94**	**98.77**	**113.54**	**150.48**	**167.97**	**148.96**	**133.82**
Books (except those purchased through book clubs)	47.81	28.73	50.62	48.71	58.42	65.09	36.31	20.39
Newspaper subscriptions	41.54	4.80	16.05	29.31	47.24	56.31	67.77	80.03
Magazine subscriptions	14.45	5.95	9.95	11.04	16.19	20.51	21.07	16.96
Newspapers, nonsubscription	9.71	4.63	8.27	10.44	11.66	12.24	9.96	6.60
Magazines, nonsubscription	7.73	7.95	8.61	8.95	9.50	7.02	5.22	3.45
Books purchased through book clubs	5.69	0.87	5.21	4.44	7.05	6.28	8.52	6.34
Telephone	**983.41**	**627.93**	**1,022.30**	**1,136.14**	**1,198.42**	**1,006.76**	**790.69**	**580.76**
Residential telephone service and pay phones	619.60	277.66	591.70	695.68	724.34	680.45	585.89	495.63
Cellular phone service	316.10	313.38	376.66	379.35	413.09	284.93	172.93	71.16
Telephones and answering machines	27.71	12.30	21.22	39.46	42.48	25.29	17.21	8.91
Phone cards	18.88	24.25	31.58	20.22	17.02	14.70	13.79	4.94
Television	**515.28**	**258.09**	**502.16**	**563.35**	**614.62**	**579.27**	**475.29**	**374.73**
Cable service and community antenna	423.79	202.60	397.00	449.26	498.11	483.61	424.22	344.12
Television sets	91.49	55.49	105.16	114.09	116.51	95.66	51.07	30.61

Note: Numbers will not add to total because not all categories are shown.
Source: Bureau of Labor Statistics, unpublished tables from the 2003 Consumer Expenditure Survey

Table 5. Information Products and Services: Indexed spending by age, 2003

(indexed average annual spending of consumer units (CU) on information products and services by age of consumer unit reference person, 2003; index definition: an index of 100 is the average for all consumer units; an index of 132 means that spending by consumer units in that group is 32 percent above the average for all consumer units; an index of 68 indicates spending that is 32 percent below the average for all consumer units)

	total consumer units	under 25	25 to 34	35 to 44	45 to 54	55 to 64	65 to 74	75+
Average spending of CU, total	$40,817	$22,396	$40,525	$47,125	$50,101	$44,191	$33,629	$25,016
Average spending of CU, index	100	55	99	116	123	108	82	61
INFORMATION SPENDING	**100**	**60**	**101**	**112**	**122**	**109**	**83**	**61**
Computer	**100**	**70**	**106**	**117**	**132**	**116**	**61**	**25**
Computers and computer hardware, nonbusiness use	100	85	111	112	133	121	52	18
Computer information services	100	51	104	122	133	109	68	34
Computer software and accessories, nonbusiness use	100	101	102	115	123	127	68	10
Repair of computer systems for nonbusiness use	100	20	65	131	140	124	117	23
Reading material	**100**	**42**	**78**	**89**	**118**	**132**	**117**	**105**
Books (except those purchased through book clubs)	100	60	106	102	122	136	76	43
Newspaper subscriptions	100	12	39	71	114	136	163	193
Magazine subscriptions	100	41	69	76	112	142	146	117
Newspapers, nonsubscription	100	48	85	108	120	126	103	68
Magazines, nonsubscription	100	103	111	116	123	91	68	45
Books purchased through book clubs	100	15	92	78	124	110	150	111
Telephone	**100**	**64**	**104**	**116**	**122**	**102**	**80**	**59**
Residential telephone service and pay phones	100	45	95	112	117	110	95	80
Cellular phone service	100	99	119	120	131	90	55	23
Telephones and answering machines	100	44	77	142	153	91	62	32
Phone cards	100	128	167	107	90	78	73	26
Television	**100**	**50**	**97**	**109**	**119**	**112**	**92**	**73**
Cable service and community antenna	100	48	94	106	118	114	100	81
Television sets	100	61	115	125	127	105	56	33

Source: Calculations by New Strategist based on the 2003 Consumer Expenditure Survey

Table 6. Information Products and Services: Total spending by age, 2003

(total annual spending on information products and services, by consumer unit (CU) age groups, 2003; numbers in thousands)

	total consumer units	under 25	25 to 34	35 to 44	45 to 54	55 to 64	65 to 74	75+
Number of consumer units	115,356	8,584	19,737	24,413	23,131	16,580	11,495	11,417
Total spending of all CUs	$4,708,523,919	$192,243,230	$799,846,267	$1,151,684,740	$1,158,882,993	$732,680,977	$386,567,309	$285,612,010
INFORMATION SPENDING	220,194,993	9,760,437	37,980,304	52,347,087	54,076,114	34,537,466	18,257,738	13,232,303
Computer	32,630,752	1,700,405	5,942,613	8,085,586	8,657,933	5,456,146	1,993,003	795,651
Computers and computer hardware, nonbusiness use	15,777,240	996,946	2,986,405	3,741,048	4,192,725	2,754,104	824,306	281,657
Computer information services	14,294,916	541,050	2,542,520	3,703,696	3,818,003	2,235,979	971,902	481,912
Computer software and accessories, nonbusiness use	2,074,101	155,113	360,200	506,081	511,658	379,682	140,469	20,893
Repair of computer systems for nonbusiness use	484,495	7,296	53,487	134,760	135,548	86,382	56,326	11,189
Reading material	14,681,358	454,437	1,949,423	2,771,852	3,480,753	2,784,943	1,712,295	1,527,823
Books (except those purchased through book clubs)	5,515,170	246,618	999,087	1,189,157	1,351,313	1,079,192	417,383	232,793
Newspaper subscriptions	4,791,888	41,203	316,779	715,545	1,092,708	933,620	779,016	913,703
Magazine subscriptions	1,666,894	51,075	196,383	269,520	374,491	340,056	242,200	193,632
Newspapers, nonsubscription	1,120,107	39,744	163,225	254,872	269,707	202,939	114,490	75,352
Magazines, nonsubscription	891,702	68,243	169,936	218,496	219,745	116,392	60,004	39,389
Books purchased through book clubs	656,376	7,468	102,830	108,394	163,074	104,122	97,937	72,384
Telephone	113,442,244	5,390,151	20,177,135	27,736,586	27,720,653	16,692,081	9,088,982	6,630,537
Residential telephone service and pay phones	71,474,578	2,383,433	11,678,383	16,983,636	16,754,709	11,281,861	6,734,806	5,658,608
Cellular phone service	36,464,032	2,690,054	7,434,138	9,261,072	9,555,185	4,724,139	1,987,830	812,434
Telephones and answering machines	3,196,515	105,583	418,819	963,337	982,605	419,308	197,829	101,725
Phone cards	2,177,921	208,162	623,294	493,631	393,690	243,726	158,516	56,400
Television	59,440,640	2,215,445	9,911,132	13,753,064	14,216,775	9,604,297	5,463,459	4,278,292
Cable service and community antenna	48,886,719	1,739,118	7,835,589	10,967,784	11,521,782	8,018,254	4,876,409	3,928,818
Television sets	10,553,920	476,326	2,075,543	2,785,279	2,694,993	1,586,043	587,050	349,474

Note: Numbers will not add to total because not all categories are shown and because of rounding.
Source: Calculations by New Strategist based on the 2003 Consumer Expenditure Survey

Table 7. Information Products and Services: Market shares by age, 2003

(percentage of total annual spending on information products and services accounted for by consumer unit age groups, 2003)

	total consumer units	under 25	25 to 34	35 to 44	45 to 54	55 to 64	65 to 74	75+
Share of total consumer units	100.0%	7.4%	17.1%	21.2%	20.1%	14.4%	10.0%	9.9%
Share of total before-tax income	100.0	3.0	16.9	25.3	26.7	16.5	6.9	4.9
Share of total spending	100.0	4.1	17.0	24.5	24.6	15.6	8.2	6.1
INFORMATION SPENDING	100.0	4.4	17.2	23.8	24.6	15.7	8.3	6.0
Computer	100.0	5.2	18.2	24.8	26.5	16.7	6.1	2.4
Computers and computer hardware, nonbusiness use	100.0	6.3	18.9	23.7	26.6	17.5	5.2	1.8
Computer information services	100.0	3.8	17.8	25.9	26.7	15.6	6.8	3.4
Computer software and accessories, nonbusiness use	100.0	7.5	17.4	24.4	24.7	18.3	6.8	1.0
Repair of computer systems for nonbusiness use	100.0	1.5	11.0	27.8	28.0	17.8	11.6	2.3
Reading material	100.0	3.1	13.3	18.9	23.7	19.0	11.7	10.4
Books (except those purchased through book clubs)	100.0	4.5	18.1	21.6	24.5	19.6	7.6	4.2
Newspaper subscriptions	100.0	0.9	6.6	14.9	22.8	19.5	16.3	19.1
Magazine subscriptions	100.0	3.1	11.8	16.2	22.5	20.4	14.5	11.6
Newspapers, nonsubscription	100.0	3.5	14.6	22.8	24.1	18.1	10.2	6.7
Magazines, nonsubscription	100.0	7.7	19.1	24.5	24.6	13.1	6.7	4.4
Books purchased through book clubs	100.0	1.1	15.7	16.5	24.8	15.9	14.9	11.0
Telephone	100.0	4.8	17.8	24.4	24.4	14.7	8.0	5.8
Residential telephone service and pay phones	100.0	3.3	16.3	23.8	23.4	15.8	9.4	7.9
Cellular phone service	100.0	7.4	20.4	25.4	26.2	13.0	5.5	2.2
Telephones and answering machines	100.0	3.3	13.1	30.1	30.7	13.1	6.2	3.2
Phone cards	100.0	9.6	28.6	22.7	18.1	11.2	7.3	2.6
Television	100.0	3.7	16.7	23.1	23.9	16.2	9.2	7.2
Cable service and community antenna	100.0	3.6	16.0	22.4	23.6	16.4	10.0	8.0
Television sets	100.0	4.5	19.7	26.4	25.5	15.0	5.6	3.3

Note: Numbers may not add to total because of rounding.
Source: Calculations by New Strategist based on the 2003 Consumer Expenditure Survey

Table 8. Information Products and Services: Average spending by income, 2003

(average annual spending on information products and services, by before-tax income of consumer units (CU), 2003; complete income reporters only)

	complete income reporters	under $20,000	$20,000– $39,999	$40,000– $49,999	$50,000– $69,999	$70,000– $79,999	$80,000– $99,999	$100,000 or more
Number of consumer units (000s)	97,391	27,100	23,941	8,891	13,890	5,121	6,909	11,537
Number of persons per CU	2.5	1.8	2.4	2.6	2.8	3.0	3.0	3.1
Average before-tax income of CU	$51,128.00	$10,752.55	$29,072.57	$44,294.00	$58,900.00	$74,560.00	$88,832.00	$154,665.00
Average spending of CU, total	42,741.66	19,862.52	31,684.32	39,756.91	49,788.99	57,128.14	65,957.39	93,514.86
INFORMATION SPENDING	**1,943.01**	**1,091.68**	**1,605.95**	**2,000.88**	**2,282.86**	**2,549.33**	**2,750.32**	**3,437.78**
Computer	**292.67**	**108.07**	**192.93**	**278.90**	**370.04**	**477.40**	**451.96**	**673.28**
Computers and computer hardware, nonbusiness use	141.82	52.67	79.88	126.48	172.64	248.50	207.20	367.93
Computer information services	127.46	46.45	94.60	134.85	171.21	191.30	211.05	249.14
Computer software and accessories, nonbusiness use	19.26	7.68	13.82	15.01	18.62	31.98	31.32	48.92
Repair of computer systems for nonbusiness use	4.13	1.27	4.63	2.56	7.57	5.62	2.39	7.29
Reading material	**133.31**	**63.96**	**99.06**	**128.78**	**143.87**	**180.44**	**202.39**	**295.78**
Books (except those purchased through book clubs)	49.82	19.46	30.38	46.04	50.51	68.57	85.72	133.70
Newspaper subscriptions	42.55	24.94	35.59	38.29	42.80	55.04	59.30	85.74
Magazine subscriptions	15.43	6.62	10.76	16.38	18.50	25.09	21.67	33.35
Newspapers, nonsubscription	10.53	6.39	10.40	11.93	13.31	12.47	10.31	15.33
Magazines, nonsubscription	8.47	3.78	6.86	7.33	9.46	12.11	13.89	17.65
Books purchased through book clubs	6.19	2.74	4.96	8.74	9.24	4.79	11.38	8.74
Telephone	**998.37**	**618.06**	**871.74**	**1,042.22**	**1,173.15**	**1,231.38**	**1,378.53**	**1,581.03**
Residential telephone service and pay phones	620.68	448.15	582.40	653.51	694.10	724.41	786.51	846.35
Cellular phone service	327.73	135.76	243.49	326.91	431.23	446.36	546.35	645.92
Telephones and answering machines	28.77	14.46	20.14	40.14	27.47	41.73	28.59	69.30
Phone cards	20.03	19.59	24.36	20.42	18.48	17.71	15.98	17.08
Television	**518.66**	**301.59**	**442.22**	**550.98**	**595.80**	**660.11**	**717.44**	**887.69**
Cable service and community antenna	428.83	270.43	385.51	468.21	510.50	523.62	561.49	640.62
Television sets	89.83	31.17	56.71	82.77	85.30	136.49	155.95	247.07

Note: Numbers will not add to total because not all categories are shown.
Source: Bureau of Labor Statistics, unpublished tables from the 2003 Consumer Expenditure Survey; calculations by New Strategist

Table 9. Information Products and Services: Indexed spending by income, 2003

(indexed average annual spending of consumer units (CU) on information products and services by before-tax income of consumer unit, 2003; complete income reporters only; index definition: an index of 100 is the average for all consumer units; an index of 132 means that spending by consumer units in that group is 32 percent above the average for all consumer units; an index of 68 indicates spending that is 32 percent below the average for all consumer units)

	complete income reporters	under $20,000	$20,000– $39,999	$40,000– $49,999	$50,000– $69,999	$70,000– $79,999	$80,000– $99,999	$100,000 or more
Average spending of CU, total	$42,742	$19,863	$31,684	$39,757	$49,789	$57,128	$65,957	$93,515
Average spending of CU, index	100	46	74	93	116	134	154	219
INFORMATION SPENDING	100	56	83	103	117	131	142	177
Computer	100	37	66	95	126	163	154	230
Computers and computer hardware, nonbusiness use	100	37	56	89	122	175	146	259
Computer information services	100	36	74	106	134	150	166	195
Computer software and accessories, nonbusiness use	100	40	72	78	97	166	163	254
Repair of computer systems for nonbusiness use	100	31	112	62	183	136	58	177
Reading material	100	48	74	97	108	135	152	222
Books (except those purchased through book clubs)	100	39	61	92	101	138	172	268
Newspaper subscriptions	100	59	84	90	101	129	139	202
Magazine subscriptions	100	43	70	106	120	163	140	216
Newspapers, nonsubscription	100	61	99	113	126	118	98	146
Magazines, nonsubscription	100	45	81	87	112	143	164	208
Books purchased through book clubs	100	44	80	141	149	77	184	141
Telephone	100	62	87	104	118	123	138	158
Residential telephone service and pay phones	100	72	94	105	112	117	127	136
Cellular phone service	100	41	74	100	132	136	167	197
Telephones and answering machines	100	50	70	140	95	145	99	241
Phone cards	100	98	122	102	92	88	80	85
Television	100	58	85	106	115	127	138	171
Cable service and community antenna	100	63	90	109	119	122	131	149
Television sets	100	35	63	92	95	152	174	275

Source: Calculations by New Strategist based on the 2003 Consumer Expenditure Survey

Table 10. Information Products and Services: Total spending by income, 2003

(total annual spending on information products and services, by before-tax income group of consumer units (CU), 2003; complete income reporters only; numbers in thousands)

	complete income reporters	under $20,000	$20,000–$39,999	$40,000–$49,999	$50,000–$69,999	$70,000–$79,999	$80,000–$99,999	$100,000 or more
Number of consumer units	97,391	27,100	23,941	8,891	13,890	5,121	6,909	11,537
Total spending of all CUs	$4,162,653,009	$538,274,380	$758,554,310	$353,478,687	$691,569,071	$292,553,205	$455,699,608	$1,078,880,940
INFORMATION SPENDING	189,231,687	29,584,615	38,448,044	17,789,824	31,708,925	13,055,119	19,001,961	39,661,668
Computer	28,503,424	2,928,819	4,618,957	2,479,700	5,139,856	2,444,765	3,122,592	7,767,631
Computers and computer hardware, nonbusiness use	13,811,992	1,427,441	1,912,451	1,124,534	2,397,970	1,272,569	1,431,545	4,244,808
Computer information services	12,413,457	1,258,763	2,264,819	1,198,951	2,378,107	979,647	1,458,144	2,874,328
Computer software and accessories, nonbusiness use	1,875,751	208,139	330,865	133,454	258,632	163,770	216,390	564,390
Repair of computer systems for nonbusiness use	402,225	34,476	110,822	22,761	105,147	28,780	16,513	84,105
Reading material	12,983,194	1,733,252	2,371,572	1,144,983	1,998,354	924,033	1,398,313	3,412,414
Books (except those purchased through book clubs)	4,852,020	527,380	727,281	409,342	701,584	351,147	592,239	1,542,497
Newspaper subscriptions	4,143,987	675,869	852,112	340,436	594,492	281,860	409,704	989,182
Magazine subscriptions	1,502,743	179,495	257,639	145,635	256,965	128,486	149,718	384,759
Newspapers, nonsubscription	1,025,527	173,290	248,980	106,070	184,876	63,859	71,232	176,862
Magazines, nonsubscription	824,902	102,515	164,201	65,171	131,399	62,015	95,966	203,628
Books purchased through book clubs	602,850	74,261	118,656	77,707	128,344	24,530	78,624	100,833
Telephone	97,232,253	16,749,380	20,870,349	9,266,378	16,295,054	6,305,897	9,524,264	18,240,343
Residential telephone service and pay phones	60,448,646	12,144,775	13,943,290	5,810,357	9,641,049	3,709,704	5,433,998	9,764,340
Cellular phone service	31,917,952	3,679,089	5,829,412	2,906,557	5,989,785	2,285,810	3,774,732	7,451,979
Telephones and answering machines	2,801,939	391,758	482,174	356,885	381,558	213,699	197,528	799,514
Phone cards	1,950,742	530,760	583,203	181,554	256,687	90,693	110,406	197,052
Television	50,512,816	8,173,164	10,587,167	4,898,763	8,275,662	3,380,423	4,956,793	10,241,280
Cable service and community antenna	41,764,183	7,328,552	9,229,502	4,162,855	7,090,845	2,681,458	3,879,334	7,390,833
Television sets	8,748,634	844,612	1,357,665	735,908	1,184,817	698,965	1,077,459	2,850,447

Note: Numbers will not add to total because not all categories are shown and because of rounding.
Source: Calculations by New Strategist based on the 2003 Consumer Expenditure Survey

Table 11. Information Products and Services: Market shares by income, 2003

(percentage of total annual spending on information products and services accounted for by before-tax income group of consumer units, 2003; complete income reporters only)

	complete income reporters	under $20,000	$20,000–$39,999	$40,000–$49,999	$50,000–$69,999	$70,000–$79,999	$80,000–$99,999	$100,000 or more
Share of total consumer units	100.0%	27.8%	24.6%	9.1%	14.3%	5.3%	7.1%	11.8%
Share of total before-tax income	100.0	5.9	14.0	7.9	16.4	7.7	12.3	35.8
Share of total spending	100.0	12.9	18.2	8.5	16.6	7.0	10.9	25.9
INFORMATION SPENDING	100.0	15.6	20.3	9.4	16.8	6.9	10.0	21.0
Computer	100.0	10.3	16.2	8.7	18.0	8.6	11.0	27.3
Computers and computer hardware, nonbusiness use	100.0	10.3	13.8	8.1	17.4	9.2	10.4	30.7
Computer information services	100.0	10.1	18.2	9.7	19.2	7.9	11.7	23.2
Computer software and accessories, nonbusiness use	100.0	11.1	17.6	7.1	13.8	8.7	11.5	30.1
Repair of computer systems for nonbusiness use	100.0	8.6	27.6	5.7	26.1	7.2	4.1	20.9
Reading material	100.0	13.3	18.3	8.8	15.4	7.1	10.8	26.3
Books (except those purchased through book clubs)	100.0	10.9	15.0	8.4	14.5	7.2	12.2	31.8
Newspaper subscriptions	100.0	16.3	20.6	8.2	14.3	6.8	9.9	23.9
Magazine subscriptions	100.0	11.9	17.1	9.7	17.1	8.6	10.0	25.6
Newspapers, nonsubscription	100.0	16.9	24.3	10.3	18.0	6.2	6.9	17.2
Magazines, nonsubscription	100.0	12.4	19.9	7.9	15.9	7.5	11.6	24.7
Books purchased through book clubs	100.0	12.3	19.7	12.9	21.3	4.1	13.0	16.7
Telephone	100.0	17.2	21.5	9.5	16.8	6.5	9.8	18.8
Residential telephone service and pay phones	100.0	20.1	23.1	9.6	15.9	6.1	9.0	16.2
Cellular phone service	100.0	11.5	18.3	9.1	18.8	7.2	11.8	23.3
Telephones and answering machines	100.0	14.0	17.2	12.7	13.6	7.6	7.0	28.5
Phone cards	100.0	27.2	29.9	9.3	13.2	4.6	5.7	10.1
Television	100.0	16.2	21.0	9.7	16.4	6.7	9.8	20.3
Cable service and community antenna	100.0	17.5	22.1	10.0	17.0	6.4	9.3	17.7
Television sets	100.0	9.7	15.5	8.4	13.5	8.0	12.3	32.6

Note: Numbers may not add to total because of rounding.
Source: Calculations by New Strategist based on the 2003 Consumer Expenditure Survey

Table 12. Information Products and Services: Average spending by high-income consumer units, 2003

(average annual spending on information products and services, by before-tax income of consumer units (CU) with high incomes, 2003; complete income reporters only)

	total complete reporters	$100,000 or more	$100,000– $119,999	$120,000– $149,999	$150,000 or more
Number of consumer units (000s)	97,391	11,537	4,384	3,151	4,002
Number of persons per CU	2.5	3.1	3.1	3.1	3.1
Average before-tax income of CU	$51,128.00	$154,665.00	$108,087.00	$131,885.00	$223,634.00
Average spending of CU, total	42,741.66	93,514.86	75,601.50	86,451.46	118,674.11
INFORMATION SPENDING	1,943.01	3,437.78	2,977.61	3,372.56	3,993.20
Computer	292.67	673.28	539.57	667.17	824.57
Computers and computer hardware, nonbusiness use	141.82	367.93	259.63	374.97	481.03
Computer information services	127.46	249.14	234.43	225.86	283.58
Computer software and accessories, nonbusiness use	19.26	48.92	39.55	58.13	51.94
Repair of computer systems for nonbusiness use	4.13	7.29	5.96	8.21	8.02
Reading material	133.31	295.78	227.78	293.31	372.22
Books (except those purchased through book clubs)	49.82	133.70	94.53	125.61	182.99
Newspaper subscriptions	42.55	85.74	71.17	84.54	102.66
Magazine subscriptions	15.43	33.35	27.11	37.09	37.25
Newspapers, nonsubscription	10.53	15.33	14.66	18.35	13.69
Magazines, nonsubscription	8.47	17.65	13.11	15.44	24.36
Books purchased through book clubs	6.19	8.74	7.08	11.38	8.47
Telephone	998.37	1,581.03	1,416.56	1,582.19	1,760.19
Residential telephone service and pay phones	620.68	846.35	756.89	836.46	952.16
Cellular phone service	327.73	645.92	607.87	635.15	696.09
Telephones and answering machines	28.77	69.30	29.00	88.49	98.22
Phone cards	20.03	17.08	19.34	20.55	11.88
Television	518.66	887.69	793.70	829.89	1,036.22
Cable service and community antenna	428.83	640.62	617.40	608.90	691.05
Television sets	89.83	247.07	176.30	220.99	345.17

Note: Numbers will not add to total because not all categories are shown.
Source: Bureau of Labor Statistics, unpublished tables from the 2003 Consumer Expenditure Survey

Table 13. Information Products and Services: Indexed spending by high-income consumer units, 2003

(indexed average annual spending of consumer units (CU) with high incomes on information products and services, by before-tax income of consumer unit, 2003; complete income reporters only; index definition: an index of 100 is the average for all consumer units; an index of 132 means that spending by consumer units in that group is 32 percent above the average for all consumer units; an index of 68 indicates spending that is 32 percent below the average for all consumer units)

	total complete reporters	$100,000 or more	$100,000–$119,999	$120,000–$149,999	$150,000 or more
Average spending of CU, total	$42,742	$93,515	$75,602	$86,451	$118,674
Average spending of CU, index	100	219	177	202	278
INFORMATION SPENDING, TOTAL	100	177	153	174	206
Computer	100	230	184	228	282
Computers and computer hardware, nonbusiness use	100	259	183	264	339
Computer information services	100	195	184	177	222
Computer software and accessories, nonbusiness use	100	254	205	302	270
Repair of computer systems for nonbusiness use	100	177	144	199	194
Reading material	100	222	171	220	279
Books (except those purchased through book clubs)	100	268	190	252	367
Newspaper subscriptions	100	202	167	199	241
Magazine subscriptions	100	216	176	240	241
Newspapers, nonsubscription	100	146	139	174	130
Magazines, nonsubscription	100	208	155	182	288
Books purchased through book clubs	100	141	114	184	137
Telephone	100	158	142	158	176
Residential telephone service and pay phones	100	136	122	135	153
Cellular phone service	100	197	185	194	212
Telephones and answering machines	100	241	101	308	341
Phone cards	100	85	97	103	59
Television	100	171	153	160	200
Cable service and community antenna	100	149	144	142	161
Television sets	100	275	196	246	384

Source: Calculations by New Strategist based on the 2003 Consumer Expenditure Survey

Table 14. Information Products and Services: Total spending by high-income consumer units, 2003

(total annual spending on information products and services, by before-tax income group of consumer units (CU) with high incomes, 2003; complete income reporters only; consumer units and dollars in thousands)

	total complete reporters	$100,000 or more	$100,000–$119,999	$120,000–$149,999	$150,000 or more
Number of consumer units	97,391	11,537	4,384	3,151	4,002
Total spending of all CUs	$4,162,653,009	$1,078,880,940	$331,436,976	$272,408,550	$474,933,788
INFORMATION SPENDING	189,231,687	39,661,668	13,053,842	10,626,937	15,980,786
Computer	28,503,424	7,767,631	2,365,475	2,102,253	3,299,929
Computers and computer hardware, nonbusiness use	13,811,992	4,244,808	1,138,218	1,181,530	1,925,082
Computer information services	12,413,457	2,874,328	1,027,741	711,685	1,134,887
Computer software and accessories, nonbusiness use	1,875,751	564,390	173,387	183,168	207,864
Repair of computer systems for nonbusiness use	402,225	84,105	26,129	25,870	32,096
Reading material	12,983,194	3,412,414	998,588	924,220	1,489,624
Books (except those purchased through book clubs)	4,852,020	1,542,497	414,420	395,797	732,326
Newspaper subscriptions	4,143,987	989,182	312,009	266,386	410,845
Magazine subscriptions	1,502,743	384,759	118,850	116,871	149,075
Newspapers, nonsubscription	1,025,527	176,862	64,269	57,821	54,787
Magazines, nonsubscription	824,902	203,628	57,474	48,651	97,489
Books purchased through book clubs	602,850	100,833	31,039	35,858	33,897
Telephone	97,232,253	18,240,343	6,210,199	4,985,481	7,044,280
Residential telephone service and pay phones	60,448,646	9,764,340	3,318,206	2,635,685	3,810,544
Cellular phone service	31,917,952	7,451,979	2,664,902	2,001,358	2,785,752
Telephones and answering machines	2,801,939	799,514	127,136	278,832	393,076
Phone cards	1,950,742	197,052	84,787	64,753	47,544
Television	50,512,816	10,241,280	3,479,581	2,614,983	4,146,952
Cable service and community antenna	41,764,183	7,390,833	2,706,682	1,918,644	2,765,582
Television sets	8,748,634	2,850,447	772,899	696,339	1,381,370

Note: Numbers will not add to total because not all categories are shown and because of rounding.
Source: Calculations by New Strategist based on the 2003 Consumer Expenditure Survey

Table 15. Information Products and Services: Market shares by high-income consumer units, 2003

(percentage of total annual spending on information products and services accounted for by before-tax income group of consumer units with high incomes, 2003; complete income reporters only)

	total complete reporters	$100,000 or more	$100,000–$119,999	$120,000–$149,999	$150,000 or more
Share of total consumer units	100.0%	11.8%	4.5%	3.2%	4.1%
Share of total before-tax income	100.0	35.8	9.5	8.3	18.0
Share of total spending	100.0	25.9	8.0	6.5	11.4
INFORMATION SPENDING	**100.0**	**21.0**	**6.9**	**5.6**	**8.4**
Computer	**100.0**	**27.3**	**8.3**	**7.4**	**11.6**
Computers and computer hardware, nonbusiness use	100.0	30.7	8.2	8.6	13.9
Computer information services	100.0	23.2	8.3	5.7	9.1
Computer software and accessories, nonbusiness use	100.0	30.1	9.2	9.8	11.1
Repair of computer systems for nonbusiness use	100.0	20.9	6.5	6.4	8.0
Reading material	**100.0**	**26.3**	**7.7**	**7.1**	**11.5**
Books (except those purchased through book clubs)	100.0	31.8	8.5	8.2	15.1
Newspaper subscriptions	100.0	23.9	7.5	6.4	9.9
Magazine subscriptions	100.0	25.6	7.9	7.8	9.9
Newspapers, nonsubscription	100.0	17.2	6.3	5.6	5.3
Magazines, nonsubscription	100.0	24.7	7.0	5.9	11.8
Books purchased through book clubs	100.0	16.7	5.1	5.9	5.6
Telephone	**100.0**	**18.8**	**6.4**	**5.1**	**7.2**
Residential telephone service and pay phones	100.0	16.2	5.5	4.4	6.3
Cellular phone service	100.0	23.3	8.3	6.3	8.7
Telephones and answering machines	100.0	28.5	4.5	10.0	14.0
Phone cards	100.0	10.1	4.3	3.3	2.4
Television	**100.0**	**20.3**	**6.9**	**5.2**	**8.2**
Cable service and community antenna	100.0	17.7	6.5	4.6	6.6
Television sets	100.0	32.6	8.8	8.0	15.8

Note: Numbers may not add to total because of rounding.
Source: Calculations by New Strategist based on the 2003 Consumer Expenditure Survey

Table 16. Information Products and Services: Average spending by household type, 2003

(average annual spending of consumer units (CU) on information products and services, by type of consumer unit, 2003)

	total consumer units	total married couples	married couples, no children	married couples with children				single parent, at least one child <18	single person
				total	oldest child under 6	oldest child 6 to 17	oldest child 18 or older		
Number of consumer units (000s)	115,356	58,448	25,132	28,584	5,496	15,047	8,041	6,999	33,929
Number of persons per CU	2.5	3.2	2.0	3.9	3.5	4.1	4.0	2.9	1.0
Average before-tax income of CU	$51,128.00	$69,472.00	$62,930.00	$75,557.00	$66,317.00	$77,508.00	$78,307.00	$29,154.00	$27,131.00
Average spending of CU, total	40,817.33	53,030.03	47,895.65	57,702.32	51,503.24	59,183.18	59,180.36	30,534.75	23,657.35
INFORMATION SPENDING	1,908.83	2,332.45	2,130.50	2,486.55	2,186.67	2,488.01	2,688.36	1,648.99	1,251.72
Computer	282.87	374.04	339.28	414.32	331.96	414.54	470.22	181.63	172.79
Computers and computer hardware, nonbusiness use	136.77	183.56	171.79	198.50	166.39	193.22	230.34	69.09	87.87
Computer information services	123.92	161.70	142.93	181.40	139.89	189.20	195.16	100.15	68.60
Computer software and accessories, nonbusiness use	17.98	23.11	20.61	26.55	22.86	26.17	29.80	10.06	13.44
Repair of computer systems for nonbusiness use	4.20	5.67	3.95	7.87	2.82	5.95	14.92	2.33	2.88
Reading material	127.27	162.81	186.42	149.49	121.09	150.52	166.98	63.96	93.09
Books (except those purchased through book clubs)	47.81	60.55	65.01	60.69	50.88	64.05	61.10	30.03	34.02
Newspaper subscriptions	41.54	56.14	70.78	45.65	33.50	42.94	59.03	11.33	29.65
Magazine subscriptions	14.45	19.08	24.03	16.01	11.68	15.81	19.34	5.91	10.26
Newspapers, nonsubscription	9.71	10.65	10.64	10.50	7.94	10.14	12.93	8.33	8.50
Magazines, nonsubscription	7.73	9.06	8.38	9.95	8.84	10.18	10.28	5.86	5.62
Books purchased through book clubs	5.69	6.75	7.44	5.91	8.08	6.03	4.22	2.49	5.02
Telephone	983.41	1,179.92	1,017.45	1,289.15	1,122.72	1,279.86	1,419.82	970.69	631.98
Residential telephone service and pay phones	619.60	724.37	662.22	757.95	650.67	761.68	824.29	636.17	429.11
Cellular phone service	316.10	399.09	311.85	471.48	419.56	451.74	543.90	281.77	179.45
Telephones and answering machines	27.71	34.53	26.61	36.85	29.01	41.98	32.13	38.39	9.32
Phone cards	18.88	20.33	15.36	21.04	21.74	22.27	18.27	13.62	13.61
Television	515.28	615.68	587.35	633.59	610.90	643.09	631.34	432.71	353.86
Cable service and community antenna	423.79	493.57	483.43	502.69	436.20	507.45	539.24	388.00	299.68
Television sets	91.49	122.11	103.92	130.90	174.70	135.64	92.10	44.71	54.18

Note: Numbers will not add to total because not all categories are shown.
Source: Bureau of Labor Statistics, unpublished data from the 2003 Consumer Expenditure Survey

Table 17. Information Products and Services: Indexed spending by household type, 2003

(indexed average annual spending of consumer units (CU) on information products and services by type of consumer unit, 2003; index definition: an index of 100 is the average for all consumer units; an index of 132 means that spending by consumer units in that group is 32 percent above the average for all consumer units; an index of 68 indicates spending that is 32 percent below the average for all consumer units)

	total consumer units	total married couples	married couples, no children	married couples with children total	oldest child under 6	oldest child 6 to 17	oldest child 18 or older	single parent, at least one child <18	single person
Average spending of CU, total	$40,817	$53,030	$47,896	$57,702	$51,503	$59,183	$59,180	$30,535	23,657
Average spending of CU, index	100	130	117	141	126	145	145	75	58
INFORMATION SPENDING	100	122	112	130	115	130	141	86	66
Computer	100	132	120	146	117	147	166	64	61
Computers and computer hardware, nonbusiness use	100	134	126	145	122	141	168	51	64
Computer information services	100	130	115	146	113	153	157	81	55
Computer software and accessories, nonbusiness use	100	129	115	148	127	146	166	56	75
Repair of computer systems for nonbusiness use	100	135	94	187	67	142	355	55	69
Reading material	100	128	146	117	95	118	131	50	73
Books (except those purchased through book clubs)	100	127	136	127	106	134	128	63	71
Newspaper subscriptions	100	135	170	110	81	103	142	27	71
Magazine subscriptions	100	132	166	111	81	109	134	41	71
Newspapers, nonsubscription	100	110	110	108	82	104	133	86	88
Magazines, nonsubscription	100	117	108	129	114	132	133	76	73
Books purchased through book clubs	100	119	131	104	142	106	74	44	88
Telephone	100	120	103	131	114	130	144	99	64
Residential telephone service and pay phones	100	117	107	122	105	123	133	103	69
Cellular phone service	100	126	99	149	133	143	172	89	57
Telephones and answering machines	100	125	96	133	105	151	116	139	34
Phone cards	100	108	81	111	115	118	97	72	72
Television	100	119	114	123	119	125	123	84	69
Cable service and community antenna	100	116	114	119	103	120	127	92	71
Television sets	100	133	114	143	191	148	101	49	59

Source: Calculations by New Strategist based on the 2003 Consumer Expenditure Survey

Table 18. Information Products and Services: Total spending by household type, 2003

(total annual spending on information products and services, by consumer unit (CU) type, 2003; numbers in thousands)

	total consumer units	total married couples	married couples, no children	married couples with children				single parent, at least one child <18	single person
				total	oldest child under 6	oldest child 6 to 17	oldest child 18 or older		
Number of consumer units	115,356	58,448	25,132	28,584	5,496	15,047	8,041	6,999	33,929
Total spending of all CUs	$4,708,523,919	$3,099,499,193	$1,203,713,476	$1,649,363,115	$283,061,807	$890,529,309	$475,869,275	$213,712,715	$802,670,228
INFORMATION SPENDING	220,194,993	136,327,038	53,543,726	71,075,545	12,017,938	37,437,086	21,617,103	11,541,281	42,469,608
Computer	32,630,752	21,861,890	8,526,785	11,842,923	1,824,452	6,237,583	3,781,039	1,271,228	5,862,592
Computers and computer hardware, nonbusiness use	15,777,240	10,728,715	4,317,426	5,673,924	914,479	2,907,381	1,852,164	483,561	2,981,341
Computer information services	14,294,916	9,451,042	3,592,117	5,185,138	768,835	2,846,892	1,569,282	700,950	2,327,529
Computer software and accessories, nonbusiness use	2,074,101	1,350,733	517,971	758,905	125,639	393,780	239,622	70,410	456,006
Repair of computer systems for nonbusiness use	484,495	331,400	99,271	224,956	15,499	89,530	119,972	16,308	97,716
Reading material	14,681,358	9,515,919	4,685,107	4,273,022	665,511	2,264,874	1,342,686	447,656	3,158,451
Books (except those purchased through book clubs)	5,515,170	3,539,026	1,633,831	1,734,763	279,636	963,760	491,305	210,180	1,154,265
Newspaper subscriptions	4,791,888	3,281,271	1,778,843	1,304,860	184,116	646,118	474,660	79,299	1,005,995
Magazine subscriptions	1,666,894	1,115,188	603,922	457,630	64,193	237,893	155,513	41,364	348,112
Newspapers, nonsubscription	1,120,107	622,471	267,404	300,132	43,638	152,577	103,970	58,302	288,397
Magazines, nonsubscription	891,702	529,539	210,606	284,411	48,585	153,178	82,661	41,014	190,681
Books purchased through book clubs	656,376	394,524	186,982	168,931	44,408	90,733	33,933	17,428	170,324
Telephone	113,442,244	68,963,964	25,570,553	36,849,064	6,170,469	19,258,053	11,416,773	6,793,859	21,442,449
Residential telephone service and pay phones	71,474,578	42,337,978	16,642,913	21,665,243	3,576,082	11,460,999	6,628,116	4,452,554	14,559,273
Cellular phone service	36,464,032	23,326,012	7,837,414	13,476,784	2,305,902	6,797,332	4,373,500	1,972,108	6,088,559
Telephones and answering machines	3,196,515	2,018,209	668,763	1,053,320	159,439	631,673	258,357	268,692	316,218
Phone cards	2,177,921	1,188,248	386,028	601,407	119,483	335,097	146,909	95,326	461,774
Television	59,440,640	35,985,265	14,761,280	18,110,537	3,357,506	9,676,575	5,076,605	3,028,537	12,006,116
Cable service and community antenna	48,886,719	28,848,179	12,149,563	14,368,891	2,397,355	7,635,600	4,336,029	2,715,612	10,167,843
Television sets	10,553,920	7,137,085	2,611,717	3,741,646	960,151	2,040,975	740,576	312,925	1,838,273

Note: Numbers will not add to total because not all categories are shown and because of rounding.
Source: Calculations by New Strategist based on the 2003 Consumer Expenditure Survey

Table 19. Information Products and Services: Market shares by household type, 2003

(percentage of total annual spending on information products and services accounted for by types of consumer units, 2003)

	total consumer units	total married couples	married couples, no children	married couples with children				single parent, at least one child <18	single person
				total	oldest child under 6	oldest child 6 to 17	oldest child 18 or older		
Share of total consumer units	100.0%	50.7%	21.8%	24.8%	4.8%	13.0%	7.0%	6.1%	29.4%
Share of total before-tax income	100.0	68.8	26.8	36.6	6.2	19.8	10.7	3.5	15.6
Share of total spending	100.0	65.8	25.6	35.0	6.0	18.9	10.1	4.5	17.0
INFORMATION SPENDING	100.0	61.9	24.3	32.3	5.5	17.0	9.8	5.2	19.3
Computer	100.0	67.0	26.1	36.3	5.6	19.1	11.6	3.9	18.0
Computers and computer hardware, nonbusiness use	100.0	68.0	27.4	36.0	5.8	18.4	11.7	3.1	18.9
Computer information services	100.0	66.1	25.1	36.3	5.4	19.9	11.0	4.9	16.3
Computer software and accessories, nonbusiness use	100.0	65.1	25.0	36.6	6.1	19.0	11.6	3.4	22.0
Repair of computer systems for nonbusiness use	100.0	68.4	20.5	46.4	3.2	18.5	24.8	3.4	20.2
Reading material	100.0	64.8	31.9	29.1	4.5	15.4	9.1	3.0	21.5
Books (except those purchased through book clubs)	100.0	64.2	29.6	31.5	5.1	17.5	8.9	3.8	20.9
Newspaper subscriptions	100.0	68.5	37.1	27.2	3.8	13.5	9.9	1.7	21.0
Magazine subscriptions	100.0	66.9	36.2	27.5	3.9	14.3	9.3	2.5	20.9
Newspapers, nonsubscription	100.0	55.6	23.9	26.8	3.9	13.6	9.3	5.2	25.7
Magazines, nonsubscription	100.0	59.4	23.6	31.9	5.4	17.2	9.3	4.6	21.4
Books purchased through book clubs	100.0	60.1	28.5	25.7	6.8	13.8	5.2	2.7	25.9
Telephone	100.0	60.8	22.5	32.5	5.4	17.0	10.1	6.0	18.9
Residential telephone service and pay phones	100.0	59.2	23.3	30.3	5.0	16.0	9.3	6.2	20.4
Cellular phone service	100.0	64.0	21.5	37.0	6.3	18.6	12.0	5.4	16.7
Telephones and answering machines	100.0	63.1	20.9	33.0	5.0	19.8	8.1	8.4	9.9
Phone cards	100.0	54.6	17.7	27.6	5.5	15.4	6.7	4.4	21.2
Television	100.0	60.5	24.8	30.5	5.6	16.3	8.5	5.1	20.2
Cable service and community antenna	100.0	59.0	24.9	29.4	4.9	15.6	8.9	5.6	20.8
Television sets	100.0	67.6	24.7	35.5	9.1	19.3	7.0	3.0	17.4

Note: Market shares by type of consumer unit will not add to total because not all types of consumer units are shown.
Source: Calculations by New Strategist based on the 2003 Consumer Expenditure Survey

Table 20. Information Products and Services: Average spending by race and Hispanic origin, 2003

(average annual spending of consumer units (CU) on information products and services, by race and Hispanic origin of consumer unit reference person, 2003)

	total consumer units	race			Hispanic origin	
		Asian	black	white and other	Hispanic	non-Hispanic
Number of consumer units (000s)	115,356	3,573	13,743	98,041	11,727	103,629
Number of persons per CU	2.5	2.8	2.6	2.5	3.3	2.4
Average before-tax income of CU	$51,128.00	$60,393.00	$34,485.00	$53,039.00	$37,150.00	$52,797.00
Average spending of CU, total	40,817.33	44,922.85	28,707.56	42,360.25	34,574.75	41,520.78
INFORMATION SPENDING	**1,908.83**	**1,922.25**	**1,718.91**	**1,934.83**	**1,613.30**	**1,942.37**
Computer	**282.87**	**341.76**	**147.23**	**299.74**	**165.96**	**296.10**
Computers and computer hardware, nonbusiness use	136.77	159.95	59.40	146.77	74.34	143.83
Computer information services	123.92	141.18	76.90	129.88	80.20	128.87
Computer software and accessories, nonbusiness use	17.98	31.39	7.39	18.98	10.39	18.84
Repair of computer systems for nonbusiness use	4.20	9.24	3.54	4.11	1.03	4.56
Reading material	**127.27**	**111.02**	**52.47**	**138.34**	**48.11**	**136.23**
Books (except those purchased through book clubs)	47.81	54.12	15.62	52.09	20.35	50.92
Newspaper subscriptions	41.54	22.96	15.70	45.85	10.23	45.09
Magazine subscriptions	14.45	12.87	4.91	15.85	4.77	15.55
Newspapers, nonsubscription	9.71	12.14	8.71	9.76	6.31	10.10
Magazines, nonsubscription	7.73	7.13	4.36	8.23	4.30	8.12
Books purchased through book clubs	5.69	1.80	3.09	6.19	2.06	6.10
Telephone	**983.41**	**1,091.66**	**1,039.03**	**971.54**	**985.97**	**983.21**
Residential telephone service and pay phones	619.60	606.32	735.73	603.81	603.22	621.45
Cellular phone service	316.10	368.46	272.11	320.36	303.30	317.55
Telephones and answering machines	27.71	65.33	12.29	28.37	18.37	28.87
Phone cards	18.88	49.30	18.15	17.87	60.09	14.21
Television	**515.28**	**377.81**	**480.18**	**525.21**	**413.26**	**526.83**
Cable service and community antenna	423.79	325.31	431.84	426.25	308.74	436.81
Television sets	91.49	52.50	48.34	98.96	104.52	90.02

Note: Other races include Alaska Natives, American Indians, Native Hawaiians, other Pacific Islanders, and consumer unit reference persons reporting more than one race. Hispanics may be of any race.
Source: Bureau of Labor Statistics, unpublished tables from the 2003 Consumer Expenditure Survey

Table 21. Information Products and Services: Indexed spending by race and Hispanic origin, 2003

(indexed average annual spending of consumer units (CU) on information products and services by race and Hispanic origin of consumer unit reference person, 2003; index definition: an index of 100 is the average for all consumer units; an index of 132 means that spending by consumer units in that group is 32 percent above the average for all consumer units; an index of 68 indicates spending that is 32 percent below the average for all consumer units)

	total consumer units	race			Hispanic origin	
		Asian	black	white and other	Hispanic	non-Hispanic
Average spending of CU, total	$40,817	$44,923	$28,708	$42,360	$34,575	$41,521
Average spending of CU, index	100	110	70	104	85	102
INFORMATION SPENDING	100	101	90	101	85	102
Computer	100	121	52	106	59	105
Computers and computer hardware, nonbusiness use	100	117	43	107	54	105
Computer information services	100	114	62	105	65	104
Computer software and accessories, nonbusiness use	100	175	41	106	58	105
Repair of computer systems for nonbusiness use	100	220	84	98	25	109
Reading material	100	87	41	109	38	107
Books (except those purchased through book clubs)	100	113	33	109	43	107
Newspaper subscriptions	100	55	38	110	25	109
Magazine subscriptions	100	89	34	110	33	108
Newspapers, nonsubscription	100	125	90	101	65	104
Magazines, nonsubscription	100	92	56	106	56	105
Books purchased through book clubs	100	32	54	109	36	107
Telephone	100	111	106	99	100	100
Residential telephone service and pay phones	100	98	119	97	97	100
Cellular phone service	100	117	86	101	96	100
Telephones and answering machines	100	236	44	102	66	104
Phone cards	100	261	96	95	318	75
Television	100	73	93	102	80	102
Cable service and community antenna	100	77	102	101	73	103
Television sets	100	57	53	108	114	98

Note: Other races include Alaska Natives, American Indians, Native Hawaiians, other Pacific Islanders, and consumer unit reference persons reporting more than one race. Hispanics may be of any race.
Source: Calculations by New Strategist based on the 2003 Consumer Expenditure Survey

Table 22. Information Products and Services: Total spending by race and Hispanic origin, 2003

(total annual spending on information products and services, by consumer unit race and Hispanic origin groups, 2003; numbers in thousands)

	total consumer units	race			Hispanic origin	
		Asian	black	white and other	Hispanic	non-Hispanic
Number of consumer units	115,356	3,573	13,743	98,041	11,727	103,629
Total spending of all consumer units	$4,708,523,919	$160,509,343	$394,527,997	$4,153,041,270	$405,458,093	$4,302,756,911
INFORMATION SPENDING	220,194,993	6,868,199	23,622,980	189,692,668	18,919,169	201,285,861
Computer	32,630,752	1,221,108	2,023,382	29,386,809	1,946,213	30,684,547
Computers and computer hardware, nonbusiness use	15,777,240	571,501	816,334	14,389,478	871,785	14,904,959
Computer information services	14,294,916	504,436	1,056,837	12,733,565	940,505	13,354,669
Computer software and accessories, nonbusiness use	2,074,101	112,156	101,561	1,860,818	121,844	1,952,370
Repair of computer systems for nonbusiness use	484,495	33,015	48,650	402,949	12,079	472,548
Reading material	14,681,358	396,674	721,095	13,562,992	564,186	14,117,379
Books (except those purchased through book clubs)	5,515,170	193,371	214,666	5,106,956	238,644	5,276,789
Newspaper subscriptions	4,791,888	82,036	215,765	4,495,180	119,967	4,672,632
Magazine subscriptions	1,666,894	45,985	67,478	1,553,950	55,938	1,611,431
Newspapers, nonsubscription	1,120,107	43,376	119,702	956,880	73,997	1,046,653
Magazines, nonsubscription	891,702	25,475	59,919	806,877	50,426	841,467
Books purchased through book clubs	656,376	6,431	42,466	606,874	24,158	632,137
Telephone	113,442,244	3,900,501	14,279,389	95,250,753	11,562,470	101,889,069
Residential telephone service and pay phones	71,474,578	2,166,381	10,111,137	59,198,136	7,073,961	64,400,242
Cellular phone service	36,464,032	1,316,508	3,739,608	31,408,415	3,556,799	32,907,389
Telephones and answering machines	3,196,515	233,424	168,901	2,781,423	215,425	2,991,769
Phone cards	2,177,921	176,149	249,435	1,751,993	704,675	1,472,568
Television	59,440,640	1,349,915	6,599,114	51,492,114	4,846,300	54,594,866
Cable service and community antenna	48,886,719	1,162,333	5,934,777	41,789,976	3,620,594	45,266,183
Television sets	10,553,920	187,583	664,337	9,702,137	1,225,706	9,328,683

Note: Other races include Alaska Natives, American Indians, Native Hawaiians, other Pacific Islanders, and consumer unit reference persons reporting more than one race. Hispanics may be of any race. Numbers will not add to total because not all categories are shown and because of rounding.
Source: Calculations by New Strategist based on the 2003 Consumer Expenditure Survey

Table 23. Information Products and Services: Market shares by race and Hispanic origin, 2003

(percentage of total annual spending on information products and services accounted for by consumer unit race and Hispanic origin groups, 2003)

	total consumer units	race			Hispanic origin	
		Asian	black	white and other	Hispanic	non-Hispanic
Share of total consumer units	100.0%	3.1%	11.9%	85.0%	10.2%	89.8%
Share of total before-tax income	100.0	3.7	8.0	88.2	7.4	92.8
Share of total spending	100.0	3.4	8.4	88.2	8.6	91.4
INFORMATION SPENDING	100.0	3.1	10.7	86.1	8.6	91.4
Computer	100.0	3.7	6.2	90.1	6.0	94.0
Computers and computer hardware, nonbusiness use	100.0	3.6	5.2	91.2	5.5	94.5
Computer information services	100.0	3.5	7.4	89.1	6.6	93.4
Computer software and accessories, nonbusiness use	100.0	5.4	4.9	89.7	5.9	94.1
Repair of computer systems for nonbusiness use	100.0	6.8	10.0	83.2	2.5	97.5
Reading material	100.0	2.7	4.9	92.4	3.8	96.2
Books (except those purchased through book clubs)	100.0	3.5	3.9	92.6	4.3	95.7
Newspaper subscriptions	100.0	1.7	4.5	93.8	2.5	97.5
Magazine subscriptions	100.0	2.8	4.0	93.2	3.4	96.7
Newspapers, nonsubscription	100.0	3.9	10.7	85.4	6.6	93.4
Magazines, nonsubscription	100.0	2.9	6.7	90.5	5.7	94.4
Books purchased through book clubs	100.0	1.0	6.5	92.5	3.7	96.3
Telephone	100.0	3.4	12.6	84.0	10.2	89.8
Residential telephone service and pay phones	100.0	3.0	14.1	82.8	9.9	90.1
Cellular phone service	100.0	3.6	10.3	86.1	9.8	90.2
Telephones and answering machines	100.0	7.3	5.3	87.0	6.7	93.6
Phone cards	100.0	8.1	11.5	80.4	32.4	67.6
Television	100.0	2.3	11.1	86.6	8.2	91.8
Cable service and community antenna	100.0	2.4	12.1	85.5	7.4	92.6
Television sets	100.0	1.8	6.3	91.9	11.6	88.4

Note: Numbers may not add to total because of rounding. Other races include Alaska Natives, American Indians, Native Hawaiians, other Pacific Islanders, and consumer unit reference persons reporting more than one race. Hispanics may be of any race. Numbers may not add to total because of rounding.
Source: Calculations by New Strategist based on the 2003 Consumer Expenditure Survey

Table 24. Information Products and Services: Average spending by region, 2003

(average annual spending of consumer units (CU) on information products and services, by region in which consumer unit lives, 2003)

	total consumer units	Northeast	Midwest	South	West
Number of consumer units (000s)	115,356	22,182	26,438	41,325	25,412
Number of persons per CU	2.5	2.4	2.5	2.5	2.6
Average before-tax income of CU	$51,128.00	$56,513.00	$52,445.00	$46,729.00	$52,506.00
Average spending of CU, total	40,817.33	42,162.29	40,280.39	37,624.55	45,380.67
INFORMATION SPENDING	**1,908.83**	**1,969.03**	**1,837.24**	**1,880.67**	**1,976.67**
Computer	**282.87**	**293.71**	**267.40**	**237.34**	**363.55**
Computers and computer hardware, nonbusiness use	136.77	141.42	127.43	104.52	194.87
Computer information services	123.92	131.33	117.28	113.52	141.27
Computer software and accessories, nonbusiness use	17.98	15.96	19.76	14.51	23.54
Repair of computer systems for nonbusiness use	4.20	5.00	2.93	4.79	3.87
Reading material	**127.27**	**153.02**	**141.14**	**93.29**	**145.61**
Books (except those purchased through book clubs)	47.81	51.82	48.82	33.75	66.13
Newspaper subscriptions	41.54	51.80	51.39	30.77	39.86
Magazine subscriptions	14.45	16.95	15.71	10.51	17.39
Newspapers, nonsubscription	9.71	17.21	10.95	6.89	6.46
Magazines, nonsubscription	7.73	7.69	8.50	6.73	8.59
Books purchased through book clubs	5.69	6.09	5.73	4.58	7.09
Telephone	**983.41**	**955.30**	**937.22**	**1,026.21**	**986.50**
Residential telephone service and pay phones	619.60	636.64	594.03	654.68	574.28
Cellular phone service	316.10	276.69	305.53	328.51	341.33
Telephones and answering machines	27.71	23.31	20.41	24.05	45.22
Phone cards	18.88	17.78	16.33	17.64	24.48
Television	**515.28**	**567.00**	**491.48**	**523.83**	**481.01**
Cable service and community antenna	423.79	478.46	409.03	435.29	372.73
Television sets	91.49	88.54	82.45	88.54	108.28

Note: Numbers will not add to total because not all categories are shown.
Source: Bureau of Labor Statistics, unpublished data from the 2003 Consumer Expenditure Survey

Table 25. Information Products and Services: Indexed spending by region, 2003

(indexed average annual spending of consumer units (CU) on information products and services by region in which consumer unit lives, 2003; index definition: an index of 100 is the average for all consumer units; an index of 132 means that spending by consumer units in that group is 32 percent above the average for all consumer units; an index of 68 indicates spending that is 32 percent below the average for all consumer units)

	total consumer units	Northeast	Midwest	South	West
Average spending of CU, total	$40,817	$42,162	$40,280	$37,625	$45,381
Average spending of CU, index	100	103	99	92	111
INFORMATION SPENDING	**100**	**103**	**96**	**99**	**104**
Computer	**100**	**104**	**95**	**84**	**129**
Computers and computer hardware, nonbusiness use	100	103	93	76	142
Computer information services	100	106	95	92	114
Computer software and accessories, nonbusiness use	100	89	110	81	131
Repair of computer systems for nonbusiness use	100	119	70	114	92
Reading material	**100**	**120**	**111**	**73**	**114**
Books (except those purchased through book clubs)	100	108	102	71	138
Newspaper subscriptions	100	125	124	74	96
Magazine subscriptions	100	117	109	73	120
Newspapers, nonsubscription	100	177	113	71	67
Magazines, nonsubscription	100	99	110	87	111
Books purchased through book clubs	100	107	101	80	125
Telephone	**100**	**97**	**95**	**104**	**100**
Residential telephone service and pay phones	100	103	96	106	93
Cellular phone service	100	88	97	104	108
Telephones and answering machines	100	84	74	87	163
Phone cards	100	94	86	93	130
Television	**100**	**110**	**95**	**102**	**93**
Cable service and community antenna	100	113	97	103	88
Television sets	100	97	90	97	118

Source: Calculations by New Strategist based on the 2003 Consumer Expenditure Survey

Table 26. Information Products and Services: Total spending by region, 2003

(total annual spending on information products and services, by region in which consumer units live, 2003; numbers in thousands)

	total consumer units	Northeast	Midwest	South	West
Number of consumer units	115,356	22,182	26,438	41,325	25,412
Total spending of all consumer units	$4,708,523,919	$935,243,917	$1,064,932,951	$1,554,834,529	$1,153,213,586
INFORMATION SPENDING	**220,194,993**	**43,677,023**	**48,572,951**	**77,718,688**	**50,231,138**
Computer	**32,630,752**	**6,515,075**	**7,069,521**	**9,808,076**	**9,238,533**
Computers and computer hardware, nonbusiness use	15,777,240	3,136,978	3,368,994	4,319,289	4,952,036
Computer information services	14,294,916	2,913,162	3,100,649	4,691,214	3,589,953
Computer software and accessories, nonbusiness use	2,074,101	354,025	522,415	599,626	598,198
Repair of computer systems for nonbusiness use	484,495	110,910	77,463	197,947	98,344
Reading material	**14,681,358**	**3,394,290**	**3,731,459**	**3,855,209**	**3,700,241**
Books (except those purchased through book clubs)	5,515,170	1,149,471	1,290,703	1,394,719	1,680,496
Newspaper subscriptions	4,791,888	1,149,028	1,358,649	1,271,570	1,012,922
Magazine subscriptions	1,666,894	375,985	415,341	434,326	441,915
Newspapers, nonsubscription	1,120,107	381,752	289,496	284,729	164,162
Magazines, nonsubscription	891,702	170,580	224,723	278,117	218,289
Books purchased through book clubs	656,376	135,088	151,490	189,269	180,171
Telephone	**113,442,244**	**21,190,465**	**24,778,222**	**42,408,128**	**25,068,938**
Residential telephone service and pay phones	71,474,578	14,121,948	15,704,965	27,054,651	14,593,603
Cellular phone service	36,464,032	6,137,538	8,077,602	13,575,676	8,673,878
Telephones and answering machines	3,196,515	517,062	539,600	993,866	1,149,131
Phone cards	2,177,921	394,396	431,733	728,973	622,086
Television	**59,440,640**	**12,577,194**	**12,993,748**	**21,647,275**	**12,223,426**
Cable service and community antenna	48,886,719	10,613,200	10,813,935	17,988,359	9,471,815
Television sets	10,553,920	1,963,994	2,179,813	3,658,916	2,751,611

Note: Numbers will not add to total because not all categories are shown and because of rounding.
Source: Calculations by New Strategist based on the 2003 Consumer Expenditure Survey

Table 27. Information Products and Services: Market shares by region, 2003

(percentage of total annual spending on information products and services accounted for by consumer units by region, 2003)

	total consumer units	Northeast	Midwest	South	West
Share of total consumer units	100.0%	19.2%	22.9%	35.8%	22.0%
Share of total before-tax income	100.0	21.5	23.4	32.8	22.5
Share of total spending	100.0	19.9	22.6	33.0	24.5
INFORMATION SPENDING	100.0	19.8	22.1	35.3	22.8
Computer	100.0	20.0	21.7	30.1	28.3
Computers and computer hardware, nonbusiness use	100.0	19.9	21.4	27.4	31.4
Computer information services	100.0	20.4	21.7	32.8	25.1
Computer software and accessories, nonbusiness use	100.0	17.1	25.2	28.9	28.8
Repair of computer systems for nonbusiness use	100.0	22.9	16.0	40.9	20.3
Reading material	100.0	23.1	25.4	26.3	25.2
Books (except those purchased through book clubs)	100.0	20.8	23.4	25.3	30.5
Newspaper subscriptions	100.0	24.0	28.4	26.5	21.1
Magazine subscriptions	100.0	22.6	24.9	26.1	26.5
Newspapers, nonsubscription	100.0	34.1	25.8	25.4	14.7
Magazines, nonsubscription	100.0	19.1	25.2	31.2	24.5
Books purchased through book clubs	100.0	20.6	23.1	28.8	27.4
Telephone	100.0	18.7	21.8	37.4	22.1
Residential telephone service and pay phones	100.0	19.8	22.0	37.9	20.4
Cellular phone service	100.0	16.8	22.2	37.2	23.8
Telephones and answering machines	100.0	16.2	16.9	31.1	35.9
Phone cards	100.0	18.1	19.8	33.5	28.6
Television	100.0	21.2	21.9	36.4	20.6
Cable service and community antenna	100.0	21.7	22.1	36.8	19.4
Television sets	100.0	18.6	20.7	34.7	26.1

Note: Numbers may not add to total because of rounding.
Source: Calculations by New Strategist based on the 2003 Consumer Expenditure Survey

Table 28. Information Products and Services: Average spending by education, 2003

(average annual spending of consumer units (CU) on information products and services, by education of consumer unit reference person, 2003)

	total consumer units	less than high school graduate	high school graduate	some college	associate's degree	college graduate total	college graduate bachelor's degree	college graduate master's, professional, doctorate
Number of consumer units (000s)	115,356	17,721	31,552	24,514	10,981	30,589	19,557	11,032
Number of persons per CU	2.5	2.6	2.5	2.3	2.6	2.5	2.5	2.4
Average before-tax income of CU	$51,128.00	$25,028.00	$40,113.00	$45,113.00	$54,087.00	$81,842.00	$74,921.00	$93,948.00
Average spending of CU, total	40,817.33	23,901.14	33,955.56	37,912.41	44,547.12	58,480.00	54,725.85	65,202.73
INFORMATION SPENDING	**1,908.83**	**1,223.91**	**1,694.49**	**1,862.05**	**2,065.19**	**2,506.21**	**2,381.53**	**2,727.99**
Computer	**282.87**	**81.40**	**184.03**	**303.93**	**304.60**	**476.86**	**436.07**	**549.18**
Computers and computer hardware, nonbusiness use	136.77	35.43	77.12	147.01	130.93	250.88	219.82	305.95
Computer information services	123.92	40.16	93.46	131.94	151.35	187.58	181.72	197.98
Computer software and accessories, nonbusiness use	17.98	5.31	8.81	19.85	17.09	33.61	29.75	40.45
Repair of computer systems for nonbusiness use	4.20	0.50	4.64	5.13	5.23	4.79	4.78	4.80
Reading material	**127.27**	**41.66**	**83.34**	**117.99**	**125.34**	**230.32**	**194.13**	**294.46**
Books (except those purchased through book clubs)	47.81	6.62	18.42	43.71	42.86	107.06	86.66	143.22
Newspaper subscriptions	41.54	21.43	35.70	37.42	39.76	63.18	54.62	78.35
Magazine subscriptions	14.45	3.07	8.82	14.16	15.14	26.85	22.20	35.09
Newspapers, nonsubscription	9.71	6.13	9.85	10.41	9.65	11.10	10.56	12.06
Magazines, nonsubscription	7.73	2.71	5.55	7.97	9.66	12.01	12.11	11.83
Books purchased through book clubs	5.69	1.67	4.94	3.91	7.74	9.49	7.28	13.40
Telephone	**983.41**	**750.45**	**917.80**	**946.09**	**1,080.47**	**1,179.22**	**1,149.01**	**1,233.53**
Residential telephone service and pay phones	619.60	551.99	609.31	572.05	661.32	692.52	679.11	716.28
Cellular phone service	316.10	146.64	272.22	338.03	373.21	421.47	410.72	440.52
Telephones and answering machines	27.71	15.67	20.66	19.84	25.31	47.25	41.66	57.92
Phone cards	18.88	35.24	14.35	15.29	18.45	17.08	16.50	18.12
Television	**515.28**	**350.40**	**509.32**	**494.04**	**554.78**	**619.81**	**602.32**	**650.82**
Cable service and community antenna	423.79	311.44	424.16	406.96	476.10	483.21	470.96	504.94
Television sets	91.49	38.96	85.16	87.08	78.68	136.60	131.36	145.88

Note: Numbers will not add to total because not all categories are shown.
Source: Bureau of Labor Statistics, unpublished data from the 2003 Consumer Expenditure Survey

Table 29. Information Products and Services: Indexed spending by education, 2003

(indexed average annual spending of consumer units (CU) on information products and services by education of consumer unit reference person, 2003; index definition: an index of 100 is the average for all consumer units; an index of 132 means that spending by consumer units in that group is 32 percent above the average for all consumer units; an index of 68 indicates spending that is 32 percent below the average for all consumer units)

	total consumer units	less than high school graduate	high school graduate	some college	associate's degree	college graduate total	college graduate bachelor's degree	college graduate master's, professional, doctorate
Average spending of CU, total	$40,817	$23,901	$33,956	$37,912	$44,547	$58,480	$54,726	$65,203
Average spending of CU, index	100	59	83	93	109	143	134	160
INFORMATION SPENDING	100	64	89	98	108	131	125	143
Computer	100	29	65	107	108	169	154	194
Computers and computer hardware, nonbusiness use	100	26	56	107	96	183	161	224
Computer information services	100	32	75	106	122	151	147	160
Computer software and accessories, nonbusiness use	100	30	49	110	95	187	165	225
Repair of computer systems for nonbusiness use	100	12	110	122	125	114	114	114
Reading material	100	33	65	93	98	181	153	231
Books (except those purchased through book clubs)	100	14	39	91	90	224	181	300
Newspaper subscriptions	100	52	86	90	96	152	131	189
Magazine subscriptions	100	21	61	98	105	186	154	243
Newspapers, nonsubscription	100	63	101	107	99	114	109	124
Magazines, nonsubscription	100	35	72	103	125	155	157	153
Books purchased through book clubs	100	29	87	69	136	167	128	236
Telephone	100	76	93	96	110	120	117	125
Residential telephone service and pay phones	100	89	98	92	107	112	110	116
Cellular phone service	100	46	86	107	118	133	130	139
Telephones and answering machines	100	57	75	72	91	171	150	209
Phone cards	100	187	76	81	98	90	87	96
Television	100	68	99	96	108	120	117	126
Cable service and community antenna	100	73	100	96	112	114	111	119
Television sets	100	43	93	95	86	149	144	159

Source: Calculations by New Strategist based on the 2003 Consumer Expenditure Survey

Table 30. Information Products and Services: Total spending by education, 2003

(total annual spending on information products and services, by consumer unit (CU) educational attainment group, 2003; numbers in thousands)

	total consumer units	less than high school graduate	high school graduate	some college	associate's degree	college graduate total	college graduate bachelor's degree	college graduate master's, professional, doctorate
Number of consumer units	115,356	17,721	31,552	24,514	10,981	30,589	19,557	11,032
Total spending of all CUs	$4,708,523,919	$423,552,102	$1,071,365,829	$929,384,819	$489,171,925	$1,788,844,720	$1,070,273,448	$719,316,517
INFORMATION SPENDING	220,194,993	21,688,909	53,464,548	45,646,294	22,677,851	76,662,458	46,575,582	30,095,186
Computer	32,630,752	1,442,489	5,806,515	7,450,540	3,344,813	14,586,671	8,528,221	6,058,554
Computers and computer hardware, nonbusiness use	15,777,240	627,855	2,433,290	3,603,803	1,437,742	7,674,168	4,299,020	3,375,240
Computer information services	14,294,916	711,675	2,948,850	3,234,377	1,661,974	5,737,885	3,553,898	2,184,115
Computer software and accessories, nonbusiness use	2,074,101	94,099	277,973	486,603	187,665	1,028,096	581,821	446,244
Repair of computer systems for nonbusiness use	484,495	8,861	146,401	125,757	57,431	146,521	93,482	52,954
Reading material	14,681,358	738,257	2,629,544	2,892,407	1,376,359	7,045,258	3,796,600	3,248,483
Books (except those purchased through book clubs)	5,515,170	117,313	581,188	1,071,507	470,646	3,274,858	1,694,810	1,580,003
Newspaper subscriptions	4,791,888	379,761	1,126,406	917,314	436,605	1,932,613	1,068,203	864,357
Magazine subscriptions	1,666,894	54,403	278,289	347,118	166,252	821,315	434,165	387,113
Newspapers, nonsubscription	1,120,107	108,630	310,787	255,191	105,967	339,538	206,522	133,046
Magazines, nonsubscription	891,702	48,024	175,114	195,377	106,076	367,374	236,835	130,509
Books purchased through book clubs	656,376	29,594	155,867	95,850	84,993	290,290	142,375	147,829
Telephone	113,442,244	13,298,724	28,958,426	23,192,450	11,864,641	36,071,161	22,471,189	13,608,303
Residential telephone service and pay phones	71,474,578	9,781,815	19,224,949	14,023,234	7,261,955	21,183,494	13,281,354	7,902,001
Cellular phone service	36,464,032	2,598,607	8,589,085	8,286,467	4,098,219	12,892,346	8,032,451	4,859,817
Telephones and answering machines	3,196,515	277,688	651,864	486,358	277,929	1,445,330	814,745	638,973
Phone cards	2,177,921	624,488	452,771	374,819	202,599	522,460	322,691	199,900
Television	59,440,640	6,209,438	16,070,065	12,110,897	6,092,039	18,959,368	11,779,572	7,179,846
Cable service and community antenna	48,886,719	5,519,028	13,383,096	9,976,217	5,228,054	14,780,911	9,210,565	5,570,498
Television sets	10,553,920	690,410	2,686,968	2,134,679	863,985	4,178,457	2,569,008	1,609,348

Note: Numbers will not add to total because not all categories are shown and because of rounding.
Source: Calculations by New Strategist based on the 2003 Consumer Expenditure Survey

Table 31. Information Products and Services: Market shares by education, 2003

(percentage of total annual spending on information products and services accounted for by consumer unit educational attainment groups, 2003)

	total consumer units	less than high school graduate	high school graduate	some college	associate's degree	college graduate total	bachelor's degree	master's, professional, doctorate
Share of total consumer units	100.0%	15.4%	27.4%	21.3%	9.5%	26.5%	17.0%	9.6%
Share of total before-tax income	100.0	7.5	21.5	18.8	10.1	42.4	24.8	17.6
Share of total spending	100.0	9.0	22.8	19.7	10.4	38.0	22.7	15.3
INFORMATION SPENDING	100.0	9.8	24.3	20.7	10.3	34.8	21.2	13.7
Computer	100.0	4.4	17.8	22.8	10.3	44.7	26.1	18.6
Computers and computer hardware, nonbusiness use	100.0	4.0	15.4	22.8	9.1	48.6	27.2	21.4
Computer information services	100.0	5.0	20.6	22.6	11.6	40.1	24.9	15.3
Computer software and accessories, nonbusiness use	100.0	4.5	13.4	23.5	9.0	49.6	28.1	21.5
Repair of computer systems for nonbusiness use	100.0	1.8	30.2	26.0	11.9	30.2	19.3	10.9
Reading material	100.0	5.0	17.9	19.7	9.4	48.0	25.9	22.1
Books (except those purchased through book clubs)	100.0	2.1	10.5	19.4	8.5	59.4	30.7	28.6
Newspaper subscriptions	100.0	7.9	23.5	19.1	9.1	40.3	22.3	18.0
Magazine subscriptions	100.0	3.3	16.7	20.8	10.0	49.3	26.0	23.2
Newspapers, nonsubscription	100.0	9.7	27.7	22.8	9.5	30.3	18.4	11.9
Magazines, nonsubscription	100.0	5.4	19.6	21.9	11.9	41.2	26.6	14.6
Books purchased through book clubs	100.0	4.5	23.7	14.6	12.9	44.2	21.7	22.5
Telephone	100.0	11.7	25.5	20.4	10.5	31.8	19.8	12.0
Residential telephone service and pay phones	100.0	13.7	26.9	19.6	10.2	29.6	18.6	11.1
Cellular phone service	100.0	7.1	23.6	22.7	11.2	35.4	22.0	13.3
Telephones and answering machines	100.0	8.7	20.4	15.2	8.7	45.2	25.5	20.0
Phone cards	100.0	28.7	20.8	17.2	9.3	24.0	14.8	9.2
Television	100.0	10.4	27.0	20.4	10.2	31.9	19.8	12.1
Cable service and community antenna	100.0	11.3	27.4	20.4	10.7	30.2	18.8	11.4
Television sets	100.0	6.5	25.5	20.2	8.2	39.6	24.3	15.2

Note: Numbers may not add to total because of rounding.
Source: Calculations by New Strategist based on the 2003 Consumer Expenditure Survey

Books (Except Those Purchased through Book Clubs)

Best customers: Householders aged 45 to 64
Married couples without children
Married couples with school-aged or older children
Households in the West
College graduates

Customer trends: Average household spending on books may rise as boomers become empty-nesters with more free time.

Book buying is the province of the highly educated. Householders with a college degree spend more than twice the average on books and account for fully 59 of the market. Householders aged 45 to 64 spend 22 to 36 percent more than average on books. Many of them are empty-nesters with time to read. Married couples without children at home (again, most of them empty-nesters) spend 36 percent more than average on this item. Couples with school-aged or older children at home spend 28 to 34 percent more than average on books because their households are relatively large.

Average household spending on books fell 10 percent between 2000 and 2003, after adjusting for inflation. This decline was far below that for newspapers or magazines and could be good news for the book industry. Books are likely to weather the Internet revolution better than other print media because there are no adequate electronic alternatives. Some of the decline in spending on books could be caused by price competition from discounters and used book sales. Average household spending on books could rise as boomers become empty-nesters with more time to read.

Table 32. Books (except those purchased through book clubs)

Total household spending $5,515,170,360.00
Average household spends 47.81

	AVERAGE HOUSEHOLD SPENDING	BEST CUSTOMERS (index)	BIGGEST CUSTOMERS (market share)
AGE OF HOUSEHOLDER			
Average household	**$47.81**	**100**	**100.0%**
Under age 25	28.73	60	4.5
Aged 25 to 34	50.62	106	18.1
Aged 35 to 44	48.71	102	21.6
Aged 45 to 54	58.42	122	24.5
Aged 55 to 64	65.09	136	19.6
Aged 65 to 74	36.31	76	7.6
Aged 75 or older	20.39	43	4.2

	AVERAGE HOUSEHOLD SPENDING	BEST CUSTOMERS (index)	BIGGEST CUSTOMERS (market share)
HOUSEHOLD INCOME			
Average household reporting income	**$49.82**	**100**	**100.0%**
Under $20,000	19.46	39	10.9
$20,000 to $39,999	30.38	61	15.0
$40,000 to $49,999	46.04	92	8.4
$50,000 to $69,999	50.51	101	14.5
$70,000 to $79,999	68.57	138	7.2
$80,000 to $99,999	85.72	172	12.2
$100,000 or more	133.70	268	31.8
HOUSEHOLD TYPE			
Average household	**47.81**	**100**	**100.0**
Married couples	60.55	127	64.2
Married couples, no children	65.01	136	29.6
Married couples, with children	60.69	127	31.5
Oldest child under 6	50.88	106	5.1
Oldest child 6 to 17	64.05	134	17.5
Oldest child 18 or older	61.10	128	8.9
Single parent with child under 18	30.03	63	3.8
Single person	34.02	71	20.9
RACE			
Average household	**47.81**	**100**	**100.0**
Asian	54.12	113	3.5
Black	15.62	33	3.9
White and other	52.09	109	92.6
HISPANIC ORIGIN			
Average household	**47.81**	**100**	**100.0**
Hispanic	20.35	43	4.3
Non-Hispanic	50.92	107	95.7
REGION			
Average household	**47.81**	**100**	**100.0**
Northeast	51.82	108	20.8
Midwest	48.82	102	23.4
South	33.75	71	25.3
West	66.13	138	30.5
EDUCATION			
Average household	**47.81**	**100**	**100.0**
Less than high school graduate	6.62	14	2.1
High school graduate	18.42	39	10.5
Some college	43.71	91	19.4
Associate's degree	42.86	90	8.5
College graduate	107.06	224	59.4
Bachelor's degree	86.66	181	30.7
Master's, professional, doctoral degree	143.22	300	28.6

Note: Market shares may not sum to 100.0 because of rounding and missing categories by household type. Other races include Alaska Natives, American Indians, Native Hawaiians, other Pacific Islanders, and consumer unit reference persons reporting more than one race. Hispanics may be of any race.
Source: Calculations by New Strategist based on the 2003 Consumer Expenditure Survey

Books Purchased through Book Clubs

Best customers: Householders aged 65 to 74
                  Married couples with preschoolers
                  Households in the West

Customer trends: Average household spending on books purchased through book clubs will continue to spiral downward as online booksellers compete on price and convenience.

The biggest spenders on books from book clubs are married couples with preschoolers, many purchasing books for their children. Couples with children under age 6 spend 42 percent more than average on this item. Households in the West spend 25 percent more. Householders aged 65 to 74 spend 50 percent more than average on this item.

Average household spending on book club books fell sharply between 2000 and 2003, down 34 percent after adjusting for inflation. Book clubs offer customers purchasing convenience and low prices. The freefall in spending on this item is a direct consequence of the convenience and low prices offered by online booksellers. This trend is likely to continue, as will the decline in average household spending on book club books.

Table 33. Books purchased through book clubs

Total household spending $656,375,640.00
Average household spends   5.69

	AVERAGE HOUSEHOLD SPENDING	BEST CUSTOMERS (index)	BIGGEST CUSTOMERS (market share)
AGE OF HOUSEHOLDER			
Average household	**$5.69**	**100**	**100.0%**
Under age 25	0.87	15	1.1
Aged 25 to 34	5.21	92	15.7
Aged 35 to 44	4.44	78	16.5
Aged 45 to 54	7.05	124	24.8
Aged 55 to 64	6.28	110	15.9
Aged 65 to 74	8.52	150	14.9
Aged 75 or older	6.34	111	11.0

	AVERAGE HOUSEHOLD SPENDING	BEST CUSTOMERS (index)	BIGGEST CUSTOMERS (market share)
HOUSEHOLD INCOME			
Average household reporting income	**$6.19**	**100**	**100.0%**
Under $20,000	2.74	44	12.3
$20,000 to $39,999	4.96	80	19.7
$40,000 to $49,999	8.74	141	12.9
$50,000 to $69,999	9.24	149	21.3
$70,000 to $79,999	4.79	77	4.1
$80,000 to $99,999	11.38	184	13.0
$100,000 or more	8.74	141	16.7
HOUSEHOLD TYPE			
Average household	**5.69**	**100**	**100.0**
Married couples	6.75	119	60.1
Married couples, no children	7.44	131	28.5
Married couples, with children	5.91	104	25.7
Oldest child under 6	8.08	142	6.8
Oldest child 6 to 17	6.03	106	13.8
Oldest child 18 or older	4.22	74	5.2
Single parent with child under 18	2.49	44	2.7
Single person	5.02	88	25.9
RACE			
Average household	**5.69**	**100**	**100.0**
Asian	1.80	32	1.0
Black	3.09	54	6.5
White and other	6.19	109	92.5
HISPANIC ORIGIN			
Average household	**5.69**	**100**	**100.0**
Hispanic	2.06	36	3.7
Non-Hispanic	6.10	107	96.3
REGION			
Average household	**5.69**	**100**	**100.0**
Northeast	6.09	107	20.6
Midwest	5.73	101	23.1
South	4.58	80	28.8
West	7.09	125	27.4
EDUCATION			
Average household	**5.69**	**100**	**100.0**
Less than high school graduate	1.67	29	4.5
High school graduate	4.94	87	23.7
Some college	3.91	69	14.6
Associate's degree	7.74	136	12.9
College graduate	9.49	167	44.2
Bachelor's degree	7.28	128	21.7
Master's, professional, doctoral degree	13.40	236	22.5

Note: Market shares may not sum to 100.0 because of rounding and missing categories by household type. Other races include Alaska Natives, American Indians, Native Hawaiians, other Pacific Islanders, and consumer unit reference persons reporting more than one race. Hispanics may be of any race.
Source: Calculations by New Strategist based on the 2003 Consumer Expenditure Survey

Cable TV or Community Antenna

Best customers: Householders aged 45 to 64
Married couples

Customer trends: Spending should stabilize along with cable TV offerings.

Cable television service has become one of the biggest household expenditures, ahead of fast-food lunches and prescription drugs. Average household spending on cable television service does not vary much by demographic characteristic. By age, the best customers are householders aged 45 to 64, spending 14 to 18 percent more than average on this item. Married couples spend 16 percent more than average on cable television. Couples with adult children at home spend 27 percent more.

Spending on cable television service grew by a substantial 23 percent between 2000 and 2003, after adjusting for inflation. Behind the increased spending on cable service is the availability of more cable channels. Many households opted for more service, with higher bills. If cable television can continue to innovate, households will continue to spend—at the expense of other entertainment categories, however.

Table 34. Cable service and community antenna

Total household spending: $48,886,719,240.00
Average household spends: 423.79

AGE OF HOUSEHOLDER	AVERAGE HOUSEHOLD SPENDING	BEST CUSTOMERS (index)	BIGGEST CUSTOMERS (market share)
Average household	$423.79	100	100.0%
Under age 25	202.60	48	3.6
Aged 25 to 34	397.00	94	16.0
Aged 35 to 44	449.26	106	22.4
Aged 45 to 54	498.11	118	23.6
Aged 55 to 64	483.61	114	16.4
Aged 65 to 74	424.22	100	10.0
Aged 75 or older	344.12	81	8.0

	AVERAGE HOUSEHOLD SPENDING	BEST CUSTOMERS (index)	BIGGEST CUSTOMERS (market share)
HOUSEHOLD INCOME			
Average household reporting income	**$428.83**	**100**	**100.0%**
Under $20,000	270.43	63	17.5
$20,000 to $39,999	385.51	90	22.1
$40,000 to $49,999	468.21	109	10.0
$50,000 to $69,999	510.50	119	17.0
$70,000 to $79,999	523.62	122	6.4
$80,000 to $99,999	561.49	131	9.3
$100,000 or more	640.62	149	17.7
HOUSEHOLD TYPE			
Average household	**423.79**	**100**	**100.0**
Married couples	493.57	116	59.0
Married couples, no children	483.43	114	24.9
Married couples, with children	502.69	119	29.4
Oldest child under 6	436.20	103	4.9
Oldest child 6 to 17	507.45	120	15.6
Oldest child 18 or older	539.24	127	8.9
Single parent with child under 18	388.00	92	5.6
Single person	299.68	71	20.8
RACE			
Average household	**423.79**	**100**	**100.0**
Asian	325.31	77	2.4
Black	431.84	102	12.1
White and other	426.25	101	85.5
HISPANIC ORIGIN			
Average household	**423.79**	**100**	**100.0**
Hispanic	308.74	73	7.4
Non-Hispanic	436.81	103	92.6
REGION			
Average household	**423.79**	**100**	**100.0**
Northeast	478.46	113	21.7
Midwest	409.03	97	22.1
South	435.29	103	36.8
West	372.73	88	19.4
EDUCATION			
Average household	**423.79**	**100**	**100.0**
Less than high school graduate	311.44	73	11.3
High school graduate	424.16	100	27.4
Some college	406.96	96	20.4
Associate's degree	476.10	112	10.7
College graduate	483.21	114	30.2
Bachelor's degree	470.96	111	18.8
Master's, professional, doctoral degree	504.94	119	11.4

Note: Market shares may not sum to 100.0 because of rounding and missing categories by household type. Other races include Alaska Natives, American Indians, Native Hawaiians, other Pacific Islanders, and consumer unit reference persons reporting more than one race. Hispanics may be of any race.
Source: Calculations by New Strategist based on the 2003 Consumer Expenditure Survey

Cellular Phone Service

Best customers: Householders aged 25 to 54
Married couples with children

Customer trends: Spending in this category should stabilize now that cell phones have become the norm and prices for cell phone service are falling.

Married couples with children are the biggest spenders on cell phone service. Couples with children spend 49 percent more than average on this item. Those with adult children at home spend 72 percent more than average. Householders aged 25 to 54, most with children at home, spend 19 to 31 percent more than average on cell phone service, controlling fully 72 percent of the market.

Average household spending on cell phone service soared between 2000 and 2003, more than doubling after adjusting for inflation. Cell phone service now ranks among the items on which households spend the most—just behind prescription drugs. The enormous growth in spending on cell phone service means slower growth in the future. Not only is cell phone service now the norm, but cutthroat competition is lowering service prices.

Table 35. Cellular phone service

Total household spending $36,464,031,600.00
Average household spends 316.10

AGE OF HOUSEHOLDER	AVERAGE HOUSEHOLD SPENDING	BEST CUSTOMERS (index)	BIGGEST CUSTOMERS (market share)
Average household	$316.10	100	100.0%
Under age 25	313.38	99	7.4
Aged 25 to 34	376.66	119	20.4
Aged 35 to 44	379.35	120	25.4
Aged 45 to 54	413.09	131	26.2
Aged 55 to 64	284.93	90	13.0
Aged 65 to 74	172.93	55	5.5
Aged 75 or older	71.16	23	2.2

	AVERAGE HOUSEHOLD SPENDING	BEST CUSTOMERS (index)	BIGGEST CUSTOMERS (market share)
HOUSEHOLD INCOME			
Average household reporting income	**$327.73**	**100**	**100.0%**
Under $20,000	135.76	41	11.5
$20,000 to $39,999	243.49	74	18.3
$40,000 to $49,999	326.91	100	9.1
$50,000 to $69,999	431.23	132	18.8
$70,000 to $79,999	446.36	136	7.2
$80,000 to $99,999	546.35	167	11.8
$100,000 or more	645.92	197	23.3
HOUSEHOLD TYPE			
Average household	**316.10**	**100**	**100.0**
Married couples	399.09	126	64.0
Married couples, no children	311.85	99	21.5
Married couples, with children	471.48	149	37.0
Oldest child under 6	419.56	133	6.3
Oldest child 6 to 17	451.74	143	18.6
Oldest child 18 or older	543.90	172	12.0
Single parent with child under 18	281.77	89	5.4
Single person	179.45	57	16.7
RACE			
Average household	**316.10**	**100**	**100.0**
Asian	368.46	117	3.6
Black	272.11	86	10.3
White and other	320.36	101	86.1
HISPANIC ORIGIN			
Average household	**316.10**	**100**	**100.0**
Hispanic	303.30	96	9.8
Non-Hispanic	317.55	100	90.2
REGION			
Average household	**316.10**	**100**	**100.0**
Northeast	276.69	88	16.8
Midwest	305.53	97	22.2
South	328.51	104	37.2
West	341.33	108	23.8
EDUCATION			
Average household	**316.10**	**100**	**100.0**
Less than high school graduate	146.64	46	7.1
High school graduate	272.22	86	23.6
Some college	338.03	107	22.7
Associate's degree	373.21	118	11.2
College graduate	421.47	133	35.4
Bachelor's degree	410.72	130	22.0
Master's, professional, doctoral degree	440.52	139	13.3

Note: Market shares may not sum to 100.0 because of rounding and missing categories by household type. Other races include Alaska Natives, American Indians, Native Hawaiians, other Pacific Islanders, and consumer unit reference persons reporting more than one race. Hispanics may be of any race.
Source: Calculations by New Strategist based on the 2003 Consumer Expenditure Survey

Computers and Computer Hardware for Nonbusiness Use

Best customers: Householders aged 45 to 54
Married couples with school-aged or older children

Customer trends: Average household spending on computers and computer hardware is likely to decline as the market becomes saturated and prices fall.

The best customers of computers and computer hardware for nonbusiness use are householders aged 45 to 54 and married couples with school-aged or older children at home. Householders aged 45 to 54 spend 33 percent more than average on computers and computer hardware. Married couples with school-aged or older children at home spend 41 to 68 percent more than the average household on this item.

Average household spending on computer hardware fell 32 percent between 2000 and 2003, after adjusting for inflation. Behind the decline is the saturation of the market as a growing majority of households became computer owners. Falling prices also contributed to the decline. These two factors will continue to influence the household market for computer hardware, pointing to a continuing decline in spending on this category.

Table 36. Computers and computer hardware for nonbusiness use

Total household spending $15,777,240,120.00
Average household spends 136.77

AGE OF HOUSEHOLDER	AVERAGE HOUSEHOLD SPENDING	BEST CUSTOMERS (index)	BIGGEST CUSTOMERS (market share)
Average household	**$136.77**	**100**	**100.0%**
Under age 25	116.14	85	6.3
Aged 25 to 34	151.31	111	18.9
Aged 35 to 44	153.24	112	23.7
Aged 45 to 54	181.26	133	26.6
Aged 55 to 64	166.11	121	17.5
Aged 65 to 74	71.71	52	5.2
Aged 75 or older	24.67	18	1.8

	AVERAGE HOUSEHOLD SPENDING	BEST CUSTOMERS (index)	BIGGEST CUSTOMERS (market share)
HOUSEHOLD INCOME			
Average household reporting income	**$141.82**	**100**	**100.0%**
Under $20,000	52.67	37	10.3
$20,000 to $39,999	79.88	56	13.8
$40,000 to $49,999	126.48	89	8.1
$50,000 to $69,999	172.64	122	17.4
$70,000 to $79,999	248.50	175	9.2
$80,000 to $99,999	207.20	146	10.4
$100,000 or more	367.93	259	30.7
HOUSEHOLD TYPE			
Average household	**136.77**	**100**	**100.0**
Married couples	183.56	134	68.0
Married couples, no children	171.79	126	27.4
Married couples, with children	198.50	145	36.0
Oldest child under 6	166.39	122	5.8
Oldest child 6 to 17	193.22	141	18.4
Oldest child 18 or older	230.34	168	11.7
Single parent with child under 18	69.09	51	3.1
Single person	87.87	64	18.9
RACE			
Average household	**136.77**	**100**	**100.0**
Asian	159.95	117	3.6
Black	59.40	43	5.2
White and other	146.77	107	91.2
HISPANIC ORIGIN			
Average household	**136.77**	**100**	**100.0**
Hispanic	74.34	54	5.5
Non-Hispanic	143.83	105	94.5
REGION			
Average household	**136.77**	**100**	**100.0**
Northeast	141.42	103	19.9
Midwest	127.43	93	21.4
South	104.52	76	27.4
West	194.87	142	31.4
EDUCATION			
Average household	**136.77**	**100**	**100.0**
Less than high school graduate	35.43	26	4.0
High school graduate	77.12	56	15.4
Some college	147.01	107	22.8
Associate's degree	130.93	96	9.1
College graduate	250.88	183	48.6
Bachelor's degree	219.82	161	27.2
Master's, professional, doctoral degree	305.95	224	21.4

Note: Market shares may not sum to 100.0 because of rounding and missing categories by household type. Other races include Alaska Natives, American Indians, Native Hawaiians, other Pacific Islanders, and consumer unit reference persons reporting more than one race. Hispanics may be of any race.
Source: Calculations by New Strategist based on the 2003 Consumer Expenditure Survey

Computer Information Services

Best customers: Householders aged 35 to 54
Married couples with school-aged or older children

Customer trends: Spending will climb as high-speed service becomes commonplace.

The best customers of computer information services (Internet access) are middle-aged, married couples with school-aged or older children at home. Married couples with school-aged or adult children at home spend 53 to 57 percent more than the average household on Internet service. Householders aged 35 to 54 spend 22 to 33 percent more than average, in large part because they are likely to be married and have children. These two age groups account for 53 percent of all household spending on Internet service.

Average household spending on computer information services grew by an impressive 89 percent between 2000 and 2003, after adjusting for inflation. The average household now spends nearly three times as much on computer information services as it does on newspaper subscriptions. Spending for online service will continue to grow as high-speed connections become commonplace and as younger generations of wired householders replace older generations with little interest in computers or Internet access.

Table 37. Computer information services

Total household spending $14,294,915,520.00
Average household spends 123.92

	AVERAGE HOUSEHOLD SPENDING	BEST CUSTOMERS (index)	BIGGEST CUSTOMERS (market share)
AGE OF HOUSEHOLDER			
Average household	**$123.92**	**100**	**100.0%**
Under age 25	63.03	51	3.8
Aged 25 to 34	128.82	104	17.8
Aged 35 to 44	151.71	122	25.9
Aged 45 to 54	165.06	133	26.7
Aged 55 to 64	134.86	109	15.6
Aged 65 to 74	84.55	68	6.8
Aged 75 or older	42.21	34	3.4

	AVERAGE HOUSEHOLD SPENDING	BEST CUSTOMERS (index)	BIGGEST CUSTOMERS (market share)
HOUSEHOLD INCOME			
Average household reporting income	**$127.46**	**100**	**100.0%**
Under $20,000	46.45	36	10.1
$20,000 to $39,999	94.60	74	18.2
$40,000 to $49,999	134.85	106	9.7
$50,000 to $69,999	171.21	134	19.2
$70,000 to $79,999	191.30	150	7.9
$80,000 to $99,999	211.05	166	11.7
$100,000 or more	249.14	195	23.2
HOUSEHOLD TYPE			
Average household	**123.92**	**100**	**100.0**
Married couples	161.70	130	66.1
Married couples, no children	142.93	115	25.1
Married couples, with children	181.40	146	36.3
Oldest child under 6	139.89	113	5.4
Oldest child 6 to 17	189.20	153	19.9
Oldest child 18 or older	195.16	157	11.0
Single parent with child under 18	100.15	81	4.9
Single person	68.60	55	16.3
RACE			
Average household	**123.92**	**100**	**100.0**
Asian	141.18	114	3.5
Black	76.90	62	7.4
White and other	129.88	105	89.1
HISPANIC ORIGIN			
Average household	**123.92**	**100**	**100.0**
Hispanic	80.20	65	6.6
Non-Hispanic	128.87	104	93.4
REGION			
Average household	**123.92**	**100**	**100.0**
Northeast	131.33	106	20.4
Midwest	117.28	95	21.7
South	113.52	92	32.8
West	141.27	114	25.1
EDUCATION			
Average household	**123.92**	**100**	**100.0**
Less than high school graduate	40.16	32	5.0
High school graduate	93.46	75	20.6
Some college	131.94	106	22.6
Associate's degree	151.35	122	11.6
College graduate	187.58	151	40.1
Bachelor's degree	181.72	147	24.9
Master's, professional, doctoral degree	197.98	160	15.3

Note: Market shares may not sum to 100.0 because of rounding and missing categories by household type. Other races include Alaska Natives, American Indians, Native Hawaiians, other Pacific Islanders, and consumer unit reference persons reporting more than one race. Hispanics may be of any race.
Source: Calculations by New Strategist based on the 2003 Consumer Expenditure Survey

Computer Software and Accessories for Nonbusiness Use

Best customers: Householders aged 35 to 64
  Married couples with children
  Asians

Customer trends: Average household spending on computer software and accessories may rebound if new applications can entice buyers.

The best customers of computer software and accessories for nonbusiness use are householders aged 35 to 64, married couples with children at home, and Asians. Householders aged 35 to 54 spend 23 to 27 percent more than the average household on computer software. Couples with children at home spend 48 percent more. Asians spend 75 percent more than average on this item.

Average household spending on computer software and accessories fell by 4 percent between 2000 and 2003, after adjusting for inflation. One factor explaining the spending decline is software bundling as manufacturers include software with their hardware in an attempt to entice buyers. Many families settle for the free software and rarely buy anything else. New must-have software applications may reverse this trend.

Table 38. Computer software and accessories for nonbusiness use

Total household spending $2,074,100,880.00
Average household spends 17.98

AGE OF HOUSEHOLDER	AVERAGE HOUSEHOLD SPENDING	BEST CUSTOMERS (index)	BIGGEST CUSTOMERS (market share)
Average household	$17.98	100	100.0%
Under age 25	18.07	101	7.5
Aged 25 to 34	18.25	102	17.4
Aged 35 to 44	20.73	115	24.4
Aged 45 to 54	22.12	123	24.7
Aged 55 to 64	22.90	127	18.3
Aged 65 to 74	12.22	68	6.8
Aged 75 or older	1.83	10	1.0

	AVERAGE HOUSEHOLD SPENDING	BEST CUSTOMERS (index)	BIGGEST CUSTOMERS (market share)
HOUSEHOLD INCOME			
Average household reporting income	**$19.26**	**100**	**100.0%**
Under $20,000	7.68	40	11.1
$20,000 to $39,999	13.82	72	17.6
$40,000 to $49,999	15.01	78	7.1
$50,000 to $69,999	18.62	97	13.8
$70,000 to $79,999	31.98	166	8.7
$80,000 to $99,999	31.32	163	11.5
$100,000 or more	48.92	254	30.1
HOUSEHOLD TYPE			
Average household	**17.98**	**100**	**100.0**
Married couples	23.11	129	65.1
Married couples, no children	20.61	115	25.0
Married couples, with children	26.55	148	36.6
Oldest child under 6	22.86	127	6.1
Oldest child 6 to 17	26.17	146	19.0
Oldest child 18 or older	29.80	166	11.6
Single parent with child under 18	10.06	56	3.4
Single person	13.44	75	22.0
RACE			
Average household	**17.98**	**100**	**100.0**
Asian	31.39	175	5.4
Black	7.39	41	4.9
White and other	18.98	106	89.7
HISPANIC ORIGIN			
Average household	**17.98**	**100**	**100.0**
Hispanic	10.39	58	5.9
Non-Hispanic	18.84	105	94.1
REGION			
Average household	**17.98**	**100**	**100.0**
Northeast	15.96	89	17.1
Midwest	19.76	110	25.2
South	14.51	81	28.9
West	23.54	131	28.8
EDUCATION			
Average household	**17.98**	**100**	**100.0**
Less than high school graduate	5.31	30	4.5
High school graduate	8.81	49	13.4
Some college	19.85	110	23.5
Associate's degree	17.09	95	9.0
College graduate	33.61	187	49.6
Bachelor's degree	29.75	165	28.1
Master's, professional, doctoral degree	40.45	225	21.5

Note: Market shares may not sum to 100.0 because of rounding and missing categories by household type. Other races include Alaska Natives, American Indians, Native Hawaiians, other Pacific Islanders, and consumer unit reference persons reporting more than one race. Hispanics may be of any race.
Source: Calculations by New Strategist based on the 2003 Consumer Expenditure Survey

Magazines, Nonsubscription

Best customers: Householders aged 25 to 54
Married couples with children

Customer trends: Average household spending on newsstand magazines will continue to decline as Internet-savvy younger generations flock to electronic alternatives.

Married couples with children are the best customers of newsstand magazines—those picked up in passing at the grocery store or airport newsstand. Householders aged 25 to 54, many with children at home, spend 11 to 23 percent more than the average household on nonsubscription magazines. Married couples with children at home spend 14 to 33 percent more than average on this item—many of them responding to their children's requests when shopping.

Average household spending on nonsubscription magazines fell a substantial 24 percent between 2000 and 2003, after adjusting for inflation. The downward trend is likely to continue as Internet-savvy younger generations flock to electronic alternatives.

Table 39. Magazines, nonsubscription

Total household spending $891,701,880.00
Average household spends 7.73

	AVERAGE HOUSEHOLD SPENDING	BEST CUSTOMERS (index)	BIGGEST CUSTOMERS (market share)
AGE OF HOUSEHOLDER			
Average household	**$7.73**	**100**	**100.0%**
Under age 25	7.95	103	7.7
Aged 25 to 34	8.61	111	19.1
Aged 35 to 44	8.95	116	24.5
Aged 45 to 54	9.50	123	24.6
Aged 55 to 64	7.02	91	13.1
Aged 65 to 74	5.22	68	6.7
Aged 75 or older	3.45	45	4.4

	AVERAGE HOUSEHOLD SPENDING	BEST CUSTOMERS (index)	BIGGEST CUSTOMERS (market share)
HOUSEHOLD INCOME			
Average household reporting income	**$8.47**	**100**	**100.0%**
Under $20,000	3.78	45	12.4
$20,000 to $39,999	6.86	81	19.9
$40,000 to $49,999	7.33	87	7.9
$50,000 to $69,999	9.46	112	15.9
$70,000 to $79,999	12.11	143	7.5
$80,000 to $99,999	13.89	164	11.6
$100,000 or more	17.65	208	24.7
HOUSEHOLD TYPE			
Average household	**7.73**	**100**	**100.0**
Married couples	9.06	117	59.4
Married couples, no children	8.38	108	23.6
Married couples, with children	9.95	129	31.9
Oldest child under 6	8.84	114	5.4
Oldest child 6 to 17	10.18	132	17.2
Oldest child 18 or older	10.28	133	9.3
Single parent with child under 18	5.86	76	4.6
Single person	5.62	73	21.4
RACE			
Average household	**7.73**	**100**	**100.0**
Asian	7.13	92	2.9
Black	4.36	56	6.7
White and other	8.23	106	90.5
HISPANIC ORIGIN			
Average household	**7.73**	**100**	**100.0**
Hispanic	4.30	56	5.7
Non-Hispanic	8.12	105	94.4
REGION			
Average household	**7.73**	**100**	**100.0**
Northeast	7.69	99	19.1
Midwest	8.50	110	25.2
South	6.73	87	31.2
West	8.59	111	24.5
EDUCATION			
Average household	**7.73**	**100**	**100.0**
Less than high school graduate	2.71	35	5.4
High school graduate	5.55	72	19.6
Some college	7.97	103	21.9
Associate's degree	9.66	125	11.9
College graduate	12.01	155	41.2
Bachelor's degree	12.11	157	26.6
Master's, professional, doctoral degree	11.83	153	14.6

Note: Market shares may not sum to 100.0 because of rounding and missing categories by household type. Other races include Alaska Natives, American Indians, Native Hawaiians, other Pacific Islanders, and consumer unit reference persons reporting more than one race. Hispanics may be of any race.
Source: Calculations by New Strategist based on the 2003 Consumer Expenditure Survey

Magazine Subscriptions

Best customers: Householders aged 55 to 74
Married couples without children

Customer trends: Average household spending on magazine subscriptions will continue to decline as Internet-savvy younger generations flock to electronic alternatives.

Older Americans are the best customers of magazine subscriptions because they have more free time and are more drawn to print than electronic media. Householders aged 55 to 74 spend 42 to 46 percent more than the average household on magazine subscriptions. Married couples without children at home (most of them empty-nesters) spend 66 percent more than average on this item.

Average household spending on magazine subscriptions fell a substantial 29 percent between 2000 and 2003, after adjusting for inflation. The downward trend is likely to continue as Internet-savvy younger generations replace older generations who prefer print.

Table 40. Magazine subscriptions

Total household spending: $1,666,894,200.00
Average household spends: 14.45

	AVERAGE HOUSEHOLD SPENDING	BEST CUSTOMERS (index)	BIGGEST CUSTOMERS (market share)
AGE OF HOUSEHOLDER			
Average household	$14.45	100	100.0%
Under age 25	5.95	41	3.1
Aged 25 to 34	9.95	69	11.8
Aged 35 to 44	11.04	76	16.2
Aged 45 to 54	16.19	112	22.5
Aged 55 to 64	20.51	142	20.4
Aged 65 to 74	21.07	146	14.5
Aged 75 or older	16.96	117	11.6

	AVERAGE HOUSEHOLD SPENDING	BEST CUSTOMERS (index)	BIGGEST CUSTOMERS (market share)
HOUSEHOLD INCOME			
Average household reporting income	**$15.43**	**100**	**100.0%**
Under $20,000	6.62	43	11.9
$20,000 to $39,999	10.76	70	17.1
$40,000 to $49,999	16.38	106	9.7
$50,000 to $69,999	18.50	120	17.1
$70,000 to $79,999	25.09	163	8.6
$80,000 to $99,999	21.67	140	10.0
$100,000 or more	33.35	216	25.6
HOUSEHOLD TYPE			
Average household	**14.45**	**100**	**100.0**
Married couples	19.08	132	66.9
Married couples, no children	24.03	166	36.2
Married couples, with children	16.01	111	27.5
Oldest child under 6	11.68	81	3.9
Oldest child 6 to 17	15.81	109	14.3
Oldest child 18 or older	19.34	134	9.3
Single parent with child under 18	5.91	41	2.5
Single person	10.26	71	20.9
RACE			
Average household	**14.45**	**100**	**100.0**
Asian	12.87	89	2.8
Black	4.91	34	4.0
White and other	15.85	110	93.2
HISPANIC ORIGIN			
Average household	**14.45**	**100**	**100.0**
Hispanic	4.77	33	3.4
Non-Hispanic	15.55	108	96.7
REGION			
Average household	**14.45**	**100**	**100.0**
Northeast	16.95	117	22.6
Midwest	15.71	109	24.9
South	10.51	73	26.1
West	17.39	120	26.5
EDUCATION			
Average household	**14.45**	**100**	**100.0**
Less than high school graduate	3.07	21	3.3
High school graduate	8.82	61	16.7
Some college	14.16	98	20.8
Associate's degree	15.14	105	10.0
College graduate	26.85	186	49.3
Bachelor's degree	22.20	154	26.0
Master's, professional, doctoral degree	35.09	243	23.2

Note: Market shares may not sum to 100.0 because of rounding and missing categories by household type. Other races include Alaska Natives, American Indians, Native Hawaiians, other Pacific Islanders, and consumer unit reference persons reporting more than one race. Hispanics may be of any race.
Source: Calculations by New Strategist based on the 2003 Consumer Expenditure Survey

Newspapers, Nonsubscription

Best customers: Householders aged 45 to 64
Married couples with adult children
Asians
Households in the Northeast

Customer trends: Average household spending on nonsubscription newspapers will continue to decline as the availability of online newspapers dampens impulse purchasing.

The best customers of nonsubscription newspapers are residents of the Northeast's commuter-friendly cities. Households in the Northeast spend 77 percent more than average on this item, many buying from newsstands or vending machines. Householders aged 45 to 64 spend 20 to 26 percent more than average on this item. Married couples with adult children at home spend 33 percent more. Asians spend 25 percent more than average on nonsubscription newspapers.

Average household spending on nonsubscription newspapers fell 26 percent between 2000 and 2003, after adjusting for inflation. The downward spiral results in part from easy (and free) access to newspapers online, dampening impulse purchasing. This trend is likely to intensify as wireless Internet access becomes more widely available to commuters and long-distance travelers.

Table 41. Newspapers, nonsubscription

Total household spending: $1,120,106,760.00
Average household spends: 9.71

	AVERAGE HOUSEHOLD SPENDING	BEST CUSTOMERS (index)	BIGGEST CUSTOMERS (market share)
AGE OF HOUSEHOLDER			
Average household	**$9.71**	**100**	**100.0%**
Under age 25	4.63	48	3.5
Aged 25 to 34	8.27	85	14.6
Aged 35 to 44	10.44	108	22.8
Aged 45 to 54	11.66	120	24.1
Aged 55 to 64	12.24	126	18.1
Aged 65 to 74	9.96	103	10.2
Aged 75 or older	6.60	68	6.7

	AVERAGE HOUSEHOLD SPENDING	BEST CUSTOMERS (index)	BIGGEST CUSTOMERS (market share)
HOUSEHOLD INCOME			
Average household reporting income	**$10.53**	**100**	**100.0%**
Under $20,000	6.39	61	16.9
$20,000 to $39,999	10.40	99	24.3
$40,000 to $49,999	11.93	113	10.3
$50,000 to $69,999	13.31	126	18.0
$70,000 to $79,999	12.47	118	6.2
$80,000 to $99,999	10.31	98	6.9
$100,000 or more	15.33	146	17.2
HOUSEHOLD TYPE			
Average household	**9.71**	**100**	**100.0**
Married couples	10.65	110	55.6
Married couples, no children	10.64	110	23.9
Married couples, with children	10.50	108	26.8
Oldest child under 6	7.94	82	3.9
Oldest child 6 to 17	10.14	104	13.6
Oldest child 18 or older	12.93	133	9.3
Single parent with child under 18	8.33	86	5.2
Single person	8.50	88	25.7
RACE			
Average household	**9.71**	**100**	**100.0**
Asian	12.14	125	3.9
Black	8.71	90	10.7
White and other	9.76	101	85.4
HISPANIC ORIGIN			
Average household	**9.71**	**100**	**100.0**
Hispanic	6.31	65	6.6
Non-Hispanic	10.10	104	93.4
REGION			
Average household	**9.71**	**100**	**100.0**
Northeast	17.21	177	34.1
Midwest	10.95	113	25.8
South	6.89	71	25.4
West	6.46	67	14.7
EDUCATION			
Average household	**9.71**	**100**	**100.0**
Less than high school graduate	6.13	63	9.7
High school graduate	9.85	101	27.7
Some college	10.41	107	22.8
Associate's degree	9.65	99	9.5
College graduate	11.10	114	30.3
Bachelor's degree	10.56	109	18.4
Master's, professional, doctoral degree	12.06	124	11.9

Note: Market shares may not sum to 100.0 because of rounding and missing categories by household type. Other races include Alaska Natives, American Indians, Native Hawaiians, other Pacific Islanders, and consumer unit reference persons reporting more than one race. Hispanics may be of any race.
Source: Calculations by New Strategist based on the 2003 Consumer Expenditure Survey

Newspaper Subscriptions

Best customers: Householders aged 55 or older
Married couples without children
Married couples with adult children

Customer trends: Average household spending on newspaper subscriptions will continue to decline as Internet-savvy younger generations flock to electronic alternatives.

Older householders are by far the best customers of newspaper subscriptions. Householders aged 55 or older spend 36 to 93 percent more than average on this item, controlling 55 percent of the market. Married couples without children at home (most of them empty-nesters) spend 70 percent more than average, while those with adult children at home spend 42 percent more.

Average household spending on newspaper subscriptions fell 18 percent between 2000 and 2003, after adjusting for inflation. The downward trend is likely to continue as Internet-savvy younger generations flock to electronic alternatives. This trend will make newspapers increasingly dependent on advertisers, rather than subscribers, for revenues.

Table 42. Newspaper subscriptions

Total household spending: $4,791,888,240.00
Average household spends: 41.54

AGE OF HOUSEHOLDER	AVERAGE HOUSEHOLD SPENDING	BEST CUSTOMERS (index)	BIGGEST CUSTOMERS (market share)
Average household	$41.54	100	100.0%
Under age 25	4.80	12	0.9
Aged 25 to 34	16.05	39	6.6
Aged 35 to 44	29.31	71	14.9
Aged 45 to 54	47.24	114	22.8
Aged 55 to 64	56.31	136	19.5
Aged 65 to 74	67.77	163	16.3
Aged 75 or older	80.03	193	19.1

	AVERAGE HOUSEHOLD SPENDING	BEST CUSTOMERS (index)	BIGGEST CUSTOMERS (market share)
HOUSEHOLD INCOME			
Average household reporting income	$42.55	100	100.0%
Under $20,000	24.94	59	16.3
$20,000 to $39,999	35.59	84	20.6
$40,000 to $49,999	38.29	90	8.2
$50,000 to $69,999	42.80	101	14.3
$70,000 to $79,999	55.04	129	6.8
$80,000 to $99,999	59.30	139	9.9
$100,000 or more	85.74	202	23.9
HOUSEHOLD TYPE			
Average household	41.54	100	100.0
Married couples	56.14	135	68.5
Married couples, no children	70.78	170	37.1
Married couples, with children	45.65	110	27.2
Oldest child under 6	33.50	81	3.8
Oldest child 6 to 17	42.94	103	13.5
Oldest child 18 or older	59.03	142	9.9
Single parent with child under 18	11.33	27	1.7
Single person	29.65	71	21.0
RACE			
Average household	41.54	100	100.0
Asian	22.96	55	1.7
Black	15.70	38	4.5
White and other	45.85	110	93.8
HISPANIC ORIGIN			
Average household	41.54	100	100.0
Hispanic	10.23	25	2.5
Non-Hispanic	45.09	109	97.5
REGION			
Average household	41.54	100	100.0
Northeast	51.80	125	24.0
Midwest	51.39	124	28.4
South	30.77	74	26.5
West	39.86	96	21.1
EDUCATION			
Average household	41.54	100	100.0
Less than high school graduate	21.43	52	7.9
High school graduate	35.70	86	23.5
Some college	37.42	90	19.1
Associate's degree	39.76	96	9.1
College graduate	63.18	152	40.3
Bachelor's degree	54.62	131	22.3
Master's, professional, doctoral degree	78.35	189	18.0

Note: Market shares may not sum to 100.0 because of rounding and missing categories by household type. Other races include Alaska Natives, American Indians, Native Hawaiians, other Pacific Islanders, and consumer unit reference persons reporting more than one race. Hispanics may be of any race.
Source: Calculations by New Strategist based on the 2003 Consumer Expenditure Survey

Phone Cards

Best customers:	Householders under age 35
	Asians and Hispanics
	Households in the West
	Householders without a high school diploma

Customer trends:	Spending in this category should grow along with the Asian and Hispanic populations.

The biggest spenders on phone cards are households without phone service and those placing international calls—primarily immigrants. Many immigrants are young adults, and many are Asian or Hispanic. This explains why householders under age 35 spend 28 to 67 percent more than average on phone cards. Asians spend more than twice the average, and Hispanics spend more than three times the average on this item. Together, Asians and Hispanics account for roughly 40 percent of the market. Households in the West spend 30 percent more than average on phone cards because the region is home to a large share of Asians and Hispanics. Householders without a high school diploma (many of them Hispanic) spend 87 percent more than average on phone cards.

Asians and Hispanics spend much more than average on phone cards because many are placing international calls and some do not have home phones. Spending on phone cards should rise along with the Asian and Hispanic populations.

Table 43. Phone cards

Total household spending	$2,177,921,280.00
Average household spends	18.88

	AVERAGE HOUSEHOLD SPENDING	BEST CUSTOMERS (index)	BIGGEST CUSTOMERS (market share)
AGE OF HOUSEHOLDER			
Average household	**$18.88**	**100**	**100.0%**
Under age 25	24.25	128	9.6
Aged 25 to 34	31.58	167	28.6
Aged 35 to 44	20.22	107	22.7
Aged 45 to 54	17.02	90	18.1
Aged 55 to 64	14.70	78	11.2
Aged 65 to 74	13.79	73	7.3
Aged 75 or older	4.94	26	2.6

	AVERAGE HOUSEHOLD SPENDING	BEST CUSTOMERS (index)	BIGGEST CUSTOMERS (market share)
HOUSEHOLD INCOME			
Average household reporting income	**$20.03**	**100**	**100.0%**
Under $20,000	19.59	98	27.2
$20,000 to $39,999	24.36	122	29.9
$40,000 to $49,999	20.42	102	9.3
$50,000 to $69,999	18.48	92	13.2
$70,000 to $79,999	17.71	88	4.6
$80,000 to $99,999	15.98	80	5.7
$100,000 or more	17.08	85	10.1
HOUSEHOLD TYPE			
Average household	**18.88**	**100**	**100.0**
Married couples	20.33	108	54.6
Married couples, no children	15.36	81	17.7
Married couples, with children	21.04	111	27.6
Oldest child under 6	21.74	115	5.5
Oldest child 6 to 17	22.27	118	15.4
Oldest child 18 or older	18.27	97	6.7
Single parent with child under 18	13.62	72	4.4
Single person	13.61	72	21.2
RACE			
Average household	**18.88**	**100**	**100.0**
Asian	49.30	261	8.1
Black	18.15	96	11.5
White and other	17.87	95	80.4
HISPANIC ORIGIN			
Average household	**18.88**	**100**	**100.0**
Hispanic	60.09	318	32.4
Non-Hispanic	14.21	75	67.6
REGION			
Average household	**18.88**	**100**	**100.0**
Northeast	17.78	94	18.1
Midwest	16.33	86	19.8
South	17.64	93	33.5
West	24.48	130	28.6
EDUCATION			
Average household	**18.88**	**100**	**100.0**
Less than high school graduate	35.24	187	28.7
High school graduate	14.35	76	20.8
Some college	15.29	81	17.2
Associate's degree	18.45	98	9.3
College graduate	17.08	90	24.0
Bachelor's degree	16.50	87	14.8
Master's, professional, doctoral degree	18.12	96	9.2

Note: Market shares may not sum to 100.0 because of rounding and missing categories by household type. Other races include Alaska Natives, American Indians, Native Hawaiians, other Pacific Islanders, and consumer unit reference persons reporting more than one race. Hispanics may be of any race.
Source: Calculations by New Strategist based on the 2003 Consumer Expenditure Survey

Residential Telephone Service and Pay Phones

Best customers: Married couples with school-aged or older children
Blacks

Customer trends: Spending in this category will decline as service prices drop and cell phones replace residential phones.

Because most households buy residential phone service, there is little variation in spending on this item by demographic characteristic. Married couples with school-aged or older children at home are the biggest spenders on residential phone service because their households are larger than average. These households spend 23 to 33 percent more than average on this item. Black households spend 19 percent more than average on residential phone service.

Average household spending on residential phone service fell 23 percent between 2000 and 2003, after adjusting for inflation. Falling service prices were behind the decline, as well as the substitution of cell phones for residential phones. Despite the decline, residential phone service still ranks among the top 15 items on which households spend the most. In the future, average household spending on residential phone service will continue to decline as cell phone service replaces residential phone service. Young adults are leading the way. Householders under age 25 cut their spending on residential phone service by 49 percent between 2000 and 2003, after adjusting for inflation.

Table 44. Residential telephone service and pay phones

Total household spending: $71,474,577,600.00
Average household spends: 619.60

	AVERAGE HOUSEHOLD SPENDING	BEST CUSTOMERS (index)	BIGGEST CUSTOMERS (market share)
AGE OF HOUSEHOLDER			
Average household	**$619.60**	**100**	**100.0%**
Under age 25	277.66	45	3.3
Aged 25 to 34	591.70	95	16.3
Aged 35 to 44	695.68	112	23.8
Aged 45 to 54	724.34	117	23.4
Aged 55 to 64	680.45	110	15.8
Aged 65 to 74	585.89	95	9.4
Aged 75 or older	495.63	80	7.9

	AVERAGE HOUSEHOLD SPENDING	BEST CUSTOMERS (index)	BIGGEST CUSTOMERS (market share)
HOUSEHOLD INCOME			
Average household reporting income	**$620.68**	**100**	**100.0%**
Under $20,000	448.15	72	20.1
$20,000 to $39,999	582.40	94	23.1
$40,000 to $49,999	653.51	105	9.6
$50,000 to $69,999	694.10	112	15.9
$70,000 to $79,999	724.41	117	6.1
$80,000 to $99,999	786.51	127	9.0
$100,000 or more	846.35	136	16.2
HOUSEHOLD TYPE			
Average household	**619.60**	**100**	**100.0**
Married couples	724.37	117	59.2
Married couples, no children	662.22	107	23.3
Married couples, with children	757.95	122	30.3
Oldest child under 6	650.67	105	5.0
Oldest child 6 to 17	761.68	123	16.0
Oldest child 18 or older	824.29	133	9.3
Single parent with child under 18	636.17	103	6.2
Single person	429.11	69	20.4
RACE			
Average household	**619.60**	**100**	**100.0**
Asian	606.32	98	3.0
Black	735.73	119	14.1
White and other	603.81	97	82.8
HISPANIC ORIGIN			
Average household	**619.60**	**100**	**100.0**
Hispanic	603.22	97	9.9
Non-Hispanic	621.45	100	90.1
REGION			
Average household	**619.60**	**100**	**100.0**
Northeast	636.64	103	19.8
Midwest	594.03	96	22.0
South	654.68	106	37.9
West	574.28	93	20.4
EDUCATION			
Average household	**619.60**	**100**	**100.0**
Less than high school graduate	551.99	89	13.7
High school graduate	609.31	98	26.9
Some college	572.05	92	19.6
Associate's degree	661.32	107	10.2
College graduate	692.52	112	29.6
Bachelor's degree	679.11	110	18.6
Master's, professional, doctoral degree	716.28	116	11.1

Note: Market shares may not sum to 100.0 because of rounding and missing categories by household type. Other races include Alaska Natives, American Indians, Native Hawaiians, other Pacific Islanders, and consumer unit reference persons reporting more than one race. Hispanics may be of any race.
Source: Calculations by New Strategist based on the 2003 Consumer Expenditure Survey

Telephones, Answering Machines, and Accessories

Best customers: Householders aged 35 to 54
Married couples with school-aged children
Single parents

Customer trends: Spending in this category may rise as cell phones turn into computers, becoming a must-have item.

The best customers of telephones, answering machines, and accessories are parents with school-aged children. Couples with children aged 6 to 17 spend 51 percent more than average on this item. Single parents spend 39 percent more. Householders aged 35 to 54, many with children at home, spend 42 to 53 percent more than average on telephones and accessories.

Average household spending on telephones, answering machines, and accessories fell 17 percent between 2000 and 2003, after adjusting for inflation. One factor behind the decline was cell phone promotions, whereby cell phone service providers gave phones away to lure customers. Falling prices for residential phones and answering machines also account for the decline. Average household spending on this item may rise in the next few years as phones evolve into computers, becoming a must-have item.

Table 45. Telephones, answering machines, and accessories

Total household spending: $3,196,514,760.00
Average household spends: 27.71

AGE OF HOUSEHOLDER	AVERAGE HOUSEHOLD SPENDING	BEST CUSTOMERS (index)	BIGGEST CUSTOMERS (market share)
Average household	$27.71	100	100.0%
Under age 25	12.30	44	3.3
Aged 25 to 34	21.22	77	13.1
Aged 35 to 44	39.46	142	30.1
Aged 45 to 54	42.48	153	30.7
Aged 55 to 64	25.29	91	13.1
Aged 65 to 74	17.21	62	6.2
Aged 75 or older	8.91	32	3.2

	AVERAGE HOUSEHOLD SPENDING	BEST CUSTOMERS (index)	BIGGEST CUSTOMERS (market share)
HOUSEHOLD INCOME			
Average household reporting income	**$28.77**	**100**	**100.0%**
Under $20,000	14.46	50	14.0
$20,000 to $39,999	20.14	70	17.2
$40,000 to $49,999	40.14	140	12.7
$50,000 to $69,999	27.47	95	13.6
$70,000 to $79,999	41.73	145	7.6
$80,000 to $99,999	28.59	99	7.0
$100,000 or more	69.30	241	28.5
HOUSEHOLD TYPE			
Average household	**27.71**	**100**	**100.0**
Married couples	34.53	125	63.1
Married couples, no children	26.61	96	20.9
Married couples, with children	36.85	133	33.0
Oldest child under 6	29.01	105	5.0
Oldest child 6 to 17	41.98	151	19.8
Oldest child 18 or older	32.13	116	8.1
Single parent with child under 18	38.39	139	8.4
Single person	9.32	34	9.9
RACE			
Average household	**27.71**	**100**	**100.0**
Asian	65.33	236	7.3
Black	12.29	44	5.3
White and other	28.37	102	87.0
HISPANIC ORIGIN			
Average household	**27.71**	**100**	**100.0**
Hispanic	18.37	66	6.7
Non-Hispanic	28.87	104	93.6
REGION			
Average household	**27.71**	**100**	**100.0**
Northeast	23.31	84	16.2
Midwest	20.41	74	16.9
South	24.05	87	31.1
West	45.22	163	35.9
EDUCATION			
Average household	**27.71**	**100**	**100.0**
Less than high school graduate	15.67	57	8.7
High school graduate	20.66	75	20.4
Some college	19.84	72	15.2
Associate's degree	25.31	91	8.7
College graduate	47.25	171	45.2
Bachelor's degree	41.66	150	25.5
Master's, professional, doctoral degree	57.92	209	20.0

Note: Market shares may not sum to 100.0 because of rounding and missing categories by household type. Other races include Alaska Natives, American Indians, Native Hawaiians, other Pacific Islanders, and consumer unit reference persons reporting more than one race. Hispanics may be of any race.
Source: Calculations by New Strategist based on the 2003 Consumer Expenditure Survey

Television Sets

Best customers: Householders aged 35 to 54
Married couples with children under age 18

Customer trends: Spending should continue to rise as more households purchase wide-screen HDTV sets.

In 2003, the best customers of television sets were householders aged 35 to 54, spending 25 to 27 percent more than average on this item. Married couples with children under age 18 spend 48 to 91 percent more than average on this item.

Average household spending on television sets grew by an impressive 33 percent between 2000 and 2003, after adjusting for inflation. Behind the increase was the growing popularity of wide-screen HDTV sets. Spending on televisions should continue to grow over the next few years as more households replace their old sets with the new technology.

Table 46. Television sets

Total household spending $10,553,920,440.00
Average household spends 91.49

AGE OF HOUSEHOLDER	AVERAGE HOUSEHOLD SPENDING	BEST CUSTOMERS (index)	BIGGEST CUSTOMERS (market share)
Average household	$91.49	100	100.0%
Under age 25	55.49	61	4.5
Aged 25 to 34	105.16	115	19.7
Aged 35 to 44	114.09	125	26.4
Aged 45 to 54	116.51	127	25.5
Aged 55 to 64	95.66	105	15.0
Aged 65 to 74	51.07	56	5.6
Aged 75 or older	30.61	33	3.3

	AVERAGE HOUSEHOLD SPENDING	BEST CUSTOMERS (index)	BIGGEST CUSTOMERS (market share)
HOUSEHOLD INCOME			
Average household reporting income	**$89.83**	**100**	**100.0%**
Under $20,000	31.17	35	9.7
$20,000 to $39,999	56.71	63	15.5
$40,000 to $49,999	82.77	92	8.4
$50,000 to $69,999	85.30	95	13.5
$70,000 to $79,999	136.49	152	8.0
$80,000 to $99,999	155.95	174	12.3
$100,000 or more	247.07	275	32.6
HOUSEHOLD TYPE			
Average household	**91.49**	**100**	**100.0**
Married couples	122.11	133	67.6
Married couples, no children	103.92	114	24.7
Married couples, with children	130.90	143	35.5
Oldest child under 6	174.70	191	9.1
Oldest child 6 to 17	135.64	148	19.3
Oldest child 18 or older	92.10	101	7.0
Single parent with child under 18	44.71	49	3.0
Single person	54.18	59	17.4
RACE			
Average household	**91.49**	**100**	**100.0**
Asian	52.50	57	1.8
Black	48.34	53	6.3
White and other	98.96	108	91.9
HISPANIC ORIGIN			
Average household	**91.49**	**100**	**100.0**
Hispanic	104.52	114	11.6
Non-Hispanic	90.02	98	88.4
REGION			
Average household	**91.49**	**100**	**100.0**
Northeast	88.54	97	18.6
Midwest	82.45	90	20.7
South	88.54	97	34.7
West	108.28	118	26.1
EDUCATION			
Average household	**91.49**	**100**	**100.0**
Less than high school graduate	38.96	43	6.5
High school graduate	85.16	93	25.5
Some college	87.08	95	20.2
Associate's degree	78.68	86	8.2
College graduate	136.60	149	39.6
Bachelor's degree	131.36	144	24.3
Master's, professional, doctoral degree	145.88	159	15.2

Note: Market shares may not sum to 100.0 because of rounding and missing categories by household type. Other races include Alaska Natives, American Indians, Native Hawaiians, other Pacific Islanders, and consumer unit reference persons reporting more than one race. Hispanics may be of any race.
Source: Calculations by New Strategist based on the 2003 Consumer Expenditure Survey

Appendix: Spending by Product and Service, 2003 Ranking

(average annual spending of consumer units on products and services, ranked by amount spent, 2003)

Mortgage interest	$2,830.50
Social Security	2,715.50
Rent	2,109.74
Federal income taxes	1,843.07
Property taxes	1,343.82
Gasoline and motor oil	1,332.76
Health insurance	1,251.62
New trucks	1,107.55
Electricity	1,027.91
New cars	944.91
Vehicle insurance	905.26
Used cars	816.42
Used trucks	795.03
Residential telephone service and pay phones	619.60
Vehicle maintenance and repairs	618.92
Cash contributions to churches, religious organizations	564.41
Apparel, women's	528.63
Dinner at full-service restaurants	517.42
Maintenance and repair services, owned homes	516.31
State and local income taxes	501.53
Pensions, deductions for private	481.22
College tuition	467.71
Cable service and community antenna	423.79
Life, endowment, annuity, other personal insurance	397.30
Natural gas	392.01
Retirement accounts, nonpayroll deposits	388.15
Vehicle finance charges	370.59
Lunch at fast-food restaurants and take-outs	369.02
Drugs, prescription	348.53
Cellular phone service	316.10
Cash gifts to nonhousehold members	301.67
Homeowner's insurance	287.43
Apparel, men's	282.18
Apparel, children's	276.76
Cigarettes	266.78
Personal care services	256.43
Airline fares	252.56
Beef	245.55
Lodging on trips	241.77
Vehicle leasing	237.19
Water and sewerage maintenance	236.30
Dental services	227.24
Dinner at fast-food restaurants and take-outs	215.93
Medicare payments	215.02
Restaurant meals on trips	213.97
Lunch at full-service restaurants	210.10
Recreation expenses on trips	195.71
Finance charges, except mortgage and vehicle	190.88
Day care centers, nurseries, and preschools	188.82
Taxes, except federal, state, and local	187.14
Snacks at fast-food restaurants and take-outs	180.26

Fresh vegetables	$171.96
Fresh fruits	170.88
Pork	170.61
Child support expenditures	166.12
Vacation homes, owned	150.29
Poultry	144.61
Physician's services	143.63
Cash contributions to charities and other organizations	139.45
Shoes, women's	138.40
Computers and computer hardware, nonbusiness use	136.77
Carbonated drinks	133.91
Laundry and cleaning supplies	132.28
Decorative items for the home	126.78
Elementary and high school tuition	124.91
Fish and seafood	124.46
Computer information services	123.92
Cosmetics, perfume, and bath products	123.43
Home equity loan, line of credit interest	122.47
Jewelry	120.16
Milk, fresh	112.58
Beer and ale at home	111.17
Legal fees	108.09
Household products, except cleaning supplies and paper products	106.32
Toys, games, hobbies, and tricycles	100.05
Pet food	99.82
Cheese	97.04
Prepared food, excluding frozen	95.13
Social, recreation, civic club membership	95.06
Housekeeping services	93.13
Breakfast at fast-food restaurants and take-outs	92.82
Sofas	92.17
Television sets	91.49
Movie, theater, opera, ballet tickets	90.69
Wine at home	89.93
Breakfast at full-service restaurants	89.42
State and local vehicle registration	88.17
Trash and garbage collection	87.63
Cereals, ready-to-eat and cooked	86.21
Camper, motorized	83.89
Gardening, lawn care service	83.70
Shoes, men's	83.38
Lawn and garden supplies	81.82
Bedroom furniture, except mattresses and springs	79.44
Fees for recreational lessons	79.36
Potato chips and other snacks	79.27
Maintenance and repair materials, owned homes	78.80
Pet purchase, supplies, and medicines	75.73
Candy and chewing gum	75.31
Cleansing and toilet tissue, paper towels, and napkins	75.23
Veterinarian services	74.18
Lunch at employer and school cafeterias	73.48
Shoes, children's	72.14
Drugs, nonprescription	70.30
Frozen prepared foods, except meals	69.94
Deductions for government retirement	69.64
Lunch meats (cold cuts)	69.31
Postage	68.94
Motorboats	65.89

Fees for participant sports	$65.73
Cash support for college students	64.39
Laundry and dry cleaning of apparel, professional	61.18
Cash contributions to educational institutions	60.37
Beer and ale at restaurants, bars	60.33
Babysitting and child care	60.04
Stationery, stationery supplies, giftwrap	59.55
Nonalcoholic beverages and ice, except fruit drinks	58.72
Ice cream and related products	58.09
Fuel oil	57.54
Funeral expenses	57.51
Vegetables, canned and dried	57.40
School lunches	56.87
Hair care products	55.65
Lawn and garden equipment	55.39
Wall units and cabinets	55.13
Books, supplies for college	54.65
Athletic gear, game tables, exercise equipment	54.52
Fruit juice, canned and bottled	53.82
Bedroom linens	53.45
Trailers and other attachable campers	53.32
Housing while attending school	52.90
Eyeglasses and contact lenses	50.97
Kitchen and dining room furniture	49.42
Bread, other than white	49.06
Mass transit fares, intracity	48.94
Catered affairs	48.39
Vitamins, nonprescription	48.02
Books, except book clubs	47.81
Refrigerators and freezers	47.56
Accounting fees	46.44
Cookies	45.06
Mattresses and springs	44.89
Hospital services other than room	43.34
Bottled/tank gas	42.42
Alimony expenditures	42.18
Newspaper subscriptions	41.54
Ground rent	40.58
Plants and fresh flowers, indoor	40.31
Living room chairs	38.76
Whiskey and other alcoholic beverages at restaurants, bars	38.75
Medical services by professionals other than physician	38.54
Sauces and gravies	38.46
Coffee	38.08
Eggs	37.34
Biscuits and rolls	37.24
Cakes and cupcakes	36.71
Laundry and dry cleaning of apparel, coin-operated	36.41
Groceries purchased on trips	36.28
Video cassettes, tapes, and discs	35.92
Rental of video cassettes, tapes, discs, films	35.76
Lottery and gambling losses	35.37
Soups, canned and packaged	35.19
Frozen meals	34.85
Occupational expenses	34.69
Eye care services	34.60
Admission to sports events	33.65
Bread, white	33.50
Records, CDs, audio tapes, needles	33.31

Wine at restaurants, bars	$18.78
Videogame hardware and software	18.70
Butter	18.08
Computer software and accessories, nonbusiness use	17.98
Tea	17.71
Living room tables	17.51
Sound components and component systems	17.47
Watches	17.12
Sugar	16.89
Maintenance and repair services, rented homes	16.88
Tolls	16.75
Train fares, intercity	16.07
Rice	16.05
Fruit, canned	15.96
Small electric kitchen appliances	15.66
Home security system service fee	15.54
Outdoor furniture	15.35
Nonelectric cookware	15.26
Curtains and draperies	15.24
Shaving products	14.80
Film	14.63
Magazine subscriptions	14.45
Hearing aids	14.40
Photographer fees	14.34
Whiskey at home	14.29
Books, supplies for elementary, high school	14.09
Laundry and cleaning equipment	14.03
Cream	13.95
Lamps and lighting fixtures	13.66
Dishwashers (built-in), garbage disposals, range hoods	13.50
Cemetery lots, vaults, and maintenance fees	13.27
Infants' equipment	13.08
Automobile service clubs	12.83
Flour mixes, prepared	12.79
Peanut butter	12.64
Office furniture for home use	12.61
Appliance repair, including service center	11.75
Olives, pickles, relishes	11.41
Termite/pest control services	11.30
Sewing materials for household items	11.27
Prepared desserts	11.10
Bicycles	11.06
Nondairy cream and imitation milk	11.02
Maintenance and repair materials, rented homes	10.23
Snacks at employer and school cafeterias	10.16
Lamb and organ meats	9.96
Pies, tarts, turnovers	9.72
Newspaper, nonsubscription	9.71
Electric personal care appliances	9.68
Tenant's insurance	9.67
Margarine	9.61
Closet and storage items	9.57
Camping equipment	9.31
Wood and other fuels	9.10
Bus fares, intercity	8.96
Sewing machines	8.95
Glassware	8.89
Vegetable juices	8.67
Vehicle inspection	8.36

Alcoholic beverages on trips	$33.26
Board (including at school)	33.25
Property management, owned home	33.03
Vehicle rental	32.95
Convalescent or nursing home care	32.80
Snacks at vending machines, mobile vendors	31.33
Hunting and fishing equipment	30.49
Cooking stoves, ovens	30.49
Moving, storage, and freight express	30.46
Electric floor-cleaning equipment	30.24
Deodorants, feminine hygiene, and misc. personal products	30.11
Topicals and dressings	30.10
Floor coverings, wall-to-wall	29.50
Lab tests, X-rays	28.93
Washing machines	28.68
Dairy, except milk, cream, and ice cream (i.e., yogurt)	28.26
Oral hygiene products	28.22
Parking fees	28.12
Ship fares	27.90
Pasta, cornmeal, and other cereal products	27.75
Sweetrolls, coffee cakes, doughnuts	27.65
Vegetables, frozen	26.79
Telephones and accessories	26.78
Baby food	26.76
Snacks at full-service restaurants	26.66
Nuts	26.41
Fats and oils	26.29
Meals as pay	26.28
Salad dressings	26.17
Photographic equipment	26.11
Hospital room	26.06
Alcoholic beverage at home, except beer, whiskey, and wine	24.70
Gifts to nonhousehold members of stocks, bonds, and mutual funds	24.68
Bakery products, frozen and refrigerated	24.56
Pet services	24.52
Crackers	24.52
Power tools	24.38
Window coverings	24.34
VCRs and video disc players	24.26
Outdoor equipment	23.74
Musical instruments and accessories	23.32
Frankfurters	22.74
Film processing	22.27
Floor coverings, nonpermanent	22.26
Taxi fares and limousine service	21.58
Tobacco products, except cigarettes	21.42
School tuition except elementary, high school, college	21.36
Jams, preserves, other sweets	21.20
Fruit juice, fresh	20.77
Salt, spices, and other seasonings	20.77
Tableware, nonelectric kitchenware	20.56
Prepared salads	20.51
Bathroom linens	20.30
Checking accounts, other bank service charges	20.01
Baking needs	19.58
Clothes dryers	19.43
Fruit-flavored drinks, noncarbonated	19.29
Phone cards	18.88

Medical equipment	$8.35
Local transportation on trips	8.33
Infants' furniture	8.17
Fruit juice, frozen	7.88
Magazines, nonsubscription	7.73
Microwave ovens	7.56
Kitchen and dining room linens	7.37
Flour	7.32
Hand tools	7.22
Driver's license	7.17
China and other dinnerware	7.04
Boat without motor and boat trailers	6.95
Portable heating and cooling equipment	6.85
Hair accessories	6.75
Cash contributions to political organizations	6.62
Silver serving pieces	6.51
Fruit, dried	6.30
Luggage	6.18
Repairs/rentals of lawn equipment, tools, etc.	6.08
Books purchased through book clubs	5.69
Artificial sweeteners	5.67
Apparel repair and tailoring	5.62
Lunch at vending machines, mobile vendors	5.56
Sound equipment accessories	5.54
Parking, owned home	5.47
Radios	5.46
Air conditioners, window	5.40
Material for making clothes	5.33
Reupholstering and furniture repair	5.20
Sewing patterns and notions	4.99
Pinball, electronic video games	4.97
Shopping club membership fees	4.92
Winter sports equipment	4.89
Delivery services	4.70
Towing charges	4.67
Water sports equipment	4.48
Compact disc, tape, record, video mail order clubs	4.38
Slipcovers and decorative pillows	4.35
Breakfast at employer and school cafeterias	4.27
Rental of recreational vehicles	4.21
Repair of computer systems for nonbusiness use	4.20
Clocks	4.02
Flatware	3.99
Tape recorders and players	3.93
Playground equipment	3.91
Fruit, frozen	3.66
Laundry and dry cleaning, nonapparel, coin-operated	3.62
Watch and jewelry repair	3.59
Docking and landing fees	3.57
Bread and cracker products	3.57
Management and upkeep services for security, owned home	3.49
Safe deposit box rental	3.48
Deductions for railroad retirement	3.42
Rental of medical equipment	3.28
Water softening service	3.23
Books, supplies for day care, nursery school	3.02
Dinner at employer and school cafeterias	2.83
Rental of furniture	2.70

Repair of TV, radio, and sound equipment	$2.60
Clothing rental	2.46
Septic tank cleaning	2.35
Credit card memberships	2.34
Fireworks	2.33
Rental and repair of musical instruments	2.29
Rental and repair of miscellaneous sports equipment	2.01
Wigs and hairpieces	1.84
Appliance rental	1.63
Plastic dinnerware	1.56
Termite/pest control products	1.52
Smoking accessories	1.42
Breakfast at vending machines, mobile vendors	1.37
Dinner at vending machines, mobile vendors	1.32
Calculators	1.27
Shoe repair and other shoe services	1.15
Smoke alarms	1.13
Pager service	1.12
Business equipment for home use	1.08
Laundry and dry cleaning, nonapparel, sent out	1.00
Telephone answering devices	0.93
Satellite dishes	0.91
School bus	0.70
Rental of television sets	0.58
Repair and rental of photographic equipment	0.58
Clothing storage	0.48
Rental of VCR, radio, sound equipment	0.29

Source: Calculations by New Strategist based on the 2003 Consumer Expenditure Survey

Glossary

age The age of the reference person, also called the householder or head of household.

average spending The average amount spent per household. The Bureau of Labor Statistics calculates the average for all households in a segment, not just for those who purchased an item. For items purchased by most households—such as bread—average spending figures are an accurate account of actual spending. For products and services purchased by few households during a year's time—such as cars—the average amount spent is much less than what purchasers spend. See the Percent Reporting table (Table 1) for the percentage of consumer units reporting an expenditure and the average amount spent by purchasers.

baby boom People born from 1946 through 1964.

baby bust People born from 1965 through 1976. Also known as generation X.

complete income reporters Respondents who provided values for major sources of income, such as wages and salaries, self-employment income, and Social Security income. Even complete income reporters may not have given a full accounting of all income from all sources.

consumer unit Defined as follows:

• All members of a household who are related by blood, marriage, adoption, or other legal arrangements.

• A person living alone or sharing a household with others or living as a roomer in a private home or lodging house or in permanent living quarters in a hotel or motel, but who is financially independent.

• Two persons or more living together who pool their income to make joint expenditure decisions. Financial independence is determined by the three major expense categories: housing, food, and other living expenses. To be considered financially independent, at least two of the three major expense categories have to be provided by the respondent. For convenience, called households in the text of this book.

consumer unit, composition of The classification of interview households by type according to: (1) relationship of other household members to the reference person; (2) age of the children to the reference person; and (3) combination of relationship to the reference person and age of the children. Stepchildren and adopted children are included with the reference person's own children.

education of reference person The number of years of formal education of the reference person based on the highest grade completed. If the respondent was enrolled at the time of interview, the grade being attended is the one recorded. Those not reporting their education are classified under no school or not reported.

expenditure The transaction cost including excise and sales taxes of goods and services acquired during the survey period. The full cost of each purchase is recorded even though full payment may not have been made at the date of purchase. Expenditure estimates include gifts. Excluded from expenditures are purchases or portions of purchases directly assignable to business purposes and periodic credit or installment payments on goods and services already acquired.

generation X People born from 1965 through 1976. Also known as the baby bust.

Hispanic origin The self-identified Hispanic origin of the consumer unit reference person. All consumer units are included in one of two Hispanic origin groups based on the reference person's Hispanic origin: Hispanic or non-Hispanic. Hispanics may be of any race.

household According to the Census Bureau, all the people who occupy a household. A group of unrelated people who share a housing unit as roommates or unmarried partners is also counted as a household. Households do not include group quarters such as college dormitories, prisons, or nursing homes. A household may contain more than one consumer unit. The terms "household" and "consumer unit" are used interchangeably in this book.

income before taxes The total money earnings and selected money receipts accruing to a consumer unit during the 12 months prior to the interview date. Income includes the following components:

• *wages and salaries* Includes total money earnings for all members of the consumer unit aged 14 or older from all jobs, including civilian wages and salaries, Armed Forces pay and allowances, piece-rate payments, commissions, tips, National Guard or Reserve pay (received for training periods), and cash bonuses before deductions for taxes, pensions, union dues, etc.

• *self-employment income* Includes net business and farm income, which consists of net income (gross receipts minus operating expenses) from a profession or unincorporated business or from the operation of a farm by an owner, tenant, or sharecropper. If the business or farm is a partnership, only an appropriate share of net income is recorded. Losses are also recorded.

• *Social Security, private and government retirement* Includes the following: payments by the federal government made under retirement, survivor, and disability insurance programs to retired persons, dependents of deceased insured workers, or to disabled workers; and private pensions or retirement benefits received by retired persons or their survivors, either directly or through an insurance company.

• *interest, dividends, rental income, and other property income* Includes interest income on savings or bonds; payments made by a corporation to its stockholders, periodic receipts from estates or trust funds; net income or loss from the rental of property, real estate, or farms, and net income or loss from roomers or boarders.

• *unemployment and workers' compensation and veterans' benefits* Includes income from unemployment compensation and workers' compensation, and veterans' payments including educational benefits, but excluding military retirement.

• *public assistance, supplemental security income, and food stamps* Includes public assistance or welfare, including that received from job training grants; supplemental security income paid by federal, state, and local welfare agencies to low-income persons who are aged 65 or older, blind, or disabled; and the value of food stamps obtained.

• *regular contributions for support* Includes alimony and child support as well as any regular contributions from persons outside the consumer unit.

• *other income* Includes money income from care of foster children, cash scholarships, fellowships, or stipends not based on working; and meals and rent as pay.

indexed spending The indexed spending figures compare the spending of each demographic segment with that of the average household. To compute an index, the amount spent on an item by a demographic segment is divided by the amount spent on the item by the average household. That figure is then multiplied by 100. An index of 100 is the average for all households. An index of 132 means average spending by households in a segment is 32 percent above average (100 plus 32). An index of 75 means average spending by households in a segment is 25 percent below average (100 minus 25). Indexed spending figures identify the consumer units that spend the most on a product or service.

market share The market share is the percentage of total household spending on an item that is accounted for by a demographic segment. Market shares are calculated by dividing a demographic segment's total spending on an item by the total spending of all households on the item. Total spending on an item for all households is calculated by multiplying average spending by the total number of households. Total spending on an item for each demographic segment is calculated by multiplying the segment's average spending by the number of households in the segment. Market shares reveal the demographic segments that account for the largest share of spending on a product or service.

millennial generation People born from 1977 through 1994.

race The self-identified race of the consumer unit reference person. All consumer units are included in one of three racial groups: Asian, black, or "white and other." The "other" group includes Alaska Natives, American Indians, Native Hawaiians, other Pacific Islanders, and persons reporting more than one race. Hispanics may be of any race.

reference person The first member mentioned by the respondent when asked to "Start with the name of the person or one of the persons who owns or rents the home." It is with respect to this person that the relationship of other consumer unit members is determined. Also called the householder or head of household.

region Consumer units are classified according to their address at the time of their participation in the survey. The four major census regions of the United States are the following state groupings:

• *Northeast:* Connecticut, Maine, Massachusetts, New Hampshire, New Jersey, New York, Pennsylvania, Rhode Island, and Vermont.

• *Midwest:* Illinois, Indiana, Iowa, Kansas, Michigan, Minnesota, Missouri, Nebraska, North Dakota, Ohio, South Dakota, and Wisconsin.

• *South:* Alabama, Arkansas, Delaware, District of Columbia, Florida, Georgia, Kentucky, Louisiana, Maryland, Mississippi, North Carolina, Oklahoma, South Carolina, Tennessee, Texas, Virginia, and West Virginia.

• *West:* Alaska, Arizona, California, Colorado, Hawaii, Idaho, Montana, Nevada, New Mexico, Oregon, Utah, Washington, and Wyoming.